A Funny Thing
Happened To Me
On My Way
To The Grave

Also by the Author:

An Autobiography

A
FUNNY THING
HAPPENED TO
ME
ON MY WAY
TO THE GRAVE

By Jack Douglas

E. P. DUTTON & CO., Inc.
New York   1962

FIRST EDITION

Published simultaneously in Canada by Clarke,
Irwin & Co., Ltd., of Toronto

LIBRARY OF CONGRESS CATALOG CARD NUMBER:
62-11321

To Reiko
Who came from heaven

via Japan Air Lines

Contents

Illustrations

A Funny Thing
Happened To Me
On My Way
To The Grave

CHAPTER 1

What Shall We Do With Your *Goddam Drum?*

THIS MORNING, while I was sitting around waiting for Reiko to bring me my Post Toasties and soy sauce, the mailman handed me a special delivery from Lynbrook. Lynbrook, Long Island, New York, which is one of my old home towns. The letter came from a Mrs. Dennis Finnegan of 1 Vincent Place in Lynbrook, an address which was familiar, because my family lived there until about thirty years ago, at which time we sold the place and moved to California. Mrs. Finnegan was writing to inform me that she and her husband were the new owners, and although the property had changed hands many times in the past thirty years, they (the Finnegans) had found something of mine in the attic: my old drum. This had led to some unpleasantness between

Mrs. Finnegan and her husband. He had wanted to keep it, but she said no. So they were leaving it up to me: "What shall we do with your goddam drum?"

⊯ ⊯ ⊯ LYNBROOK, WHEN WE LIVED there, was quite rural, and there was not much excitement. About the only fun we had was watching railroad crossing accidents. Railroad crossing accidents to Long Islanders were like barn-raisings to Pennsylvanians. They brought the whole community together at least once a week. And some times oftener in Lynbrook, because Lynbrook was happily situated astride two branch lines, and if you were personally involved in one of these "spectaculars" you had a choice of meeting your maker by steam train, on the Babylon Branch or electric on the Long Beach branch—or both, if the stars were right. Of course, now, people no longer need the Long Island railroad to get killed. They have each other.

We lived in a house that my father had had built. It was a two-story house with three bedrooms upstairs, and a living room, sun porch and kitchen downstairs. The telephone, I remember, was on the landing, halfway between upstairs and downstairs, so that it would be handy to both. Actually it was *un*handy to both, but we mustn't forget that we were pioneers and we had to rough it, with no extensions or Princess phones or anything. We didn't have television either. All we had was a superheterodyne wireless set that my mother used to sit at all night long, twisting hundreds of dials, trying to get "distance" stations. One night—or I should say at three o'clock one morning—she got KFI in Los

Angeles. On the verge of hysteria, she woke the rest of us up and we all took turns listening (with ear phones), and sure enough it was KFI, Los Angeles, and they had a mixed chorus singing "All the World Is Waiting for the Sunrise." Immediately she sat down and wrote KFI a letter telling them what she had heard and at what time, and after a while she received a "verification" stamp from KFI, and Mother was ecstatic. Sounds like it didn't take much to make Mother ecstatic, doesn't it? But it really was quite an achievement, because it meant many hours of cat-whisker tuning to bring in a station 2475 miles away and with only (in those days) 1500 watts of power. Later, of course, when my mother and father moved to California, KFI was a helluva lot harder to get.

When I was twelve years old, Lynbrook was still more country than suburban, so I became a mushratter; that is, I trapped mushrats in the swamps a little south of Lynbrook, in the township of East Rockaway, which was then nothing but swamps. Today it's a development. Mushratting was very dangerous for the mushratter as well as for the mush-rats, because you had to be out in the swamps at three o'clock in the morning to check your traps before the mush-rats gnawed off their own legs and escaped. Wandering around a swamp alone, at three a.m. on a below zero winter's morning, wasn't the brightest thing in the world to do. You could step into a hole and disappear from view forever, or you could step into a *mushrat's* trap and have to gnaw off your *own* leg and escape before the mushrat came to check *his* trap.

This sort of thing could *really* spoil your breakfast. However, in the four or five years that I trapped mushrats in the swamps, nothing ever happened to me, except one night I met Emily Brontë with a bagful of mushrats and a notebook. Shook me up. Her, too.

We had quite a few celebrities in and around Lynbrook. Gilda Gray lived in nearby Oceanside. The roof of her house was covered with stuffed cats, but I never found out why. Gilda's house is now an undertaker's. I haven't seen it lately, but I imagine the stuffed cats are gone. Then again, maybe not; there are quite a few hip undertakers around these days. A few blocks away, Eddie Leonard had a home. Eddie Leonard was a very famous song and dance man in his day, and his day must have been quite a long time ago because even *then* nobody knew who he was. Frank Tinney, who was a famous comedian, lived in another nearby town: Freeport. Frank Tinney got himself out of show business suddenly one night by the simple trick of beating up some blonde. Everybody went "tsk! tsk! tsk!" and from then on nobody went to see his shows, and that was that. The only other celebrity I can remember at the moment is Gordy Murdock. Gordy Murdock was a red-hot celebrity for a few days. Gordy stuck up a Long Island railroad mail car one night. He was caught the next day with the loot stashed under the seat of his coal delivery truck, and his excuse because he wanted new seat covers, didn't prevent him from being prosecuted. I don't know how long they gave him, but he was still away by the time I left town. Gordy should really *still* be a red-hot celebrity, because this was actually the *very last* bona fide mail car robbery in the whole United States. How about a TV series, Manny?

My mother, who was English, was very dark, looked like a gypsy and was a bit eccentric, although *she* never thought so. She loved dogs. Especially German shepherds, and we had quite a few, all of them the most vicious animals, outside of a Nazi SS group, I've ever seen. None of us could ever figure out why they were so ferocious. They certainly weren't trained to be, but somehow they turned out that way. One in particular, Peter we called him, was a real nut. Every time you walked into the kitchen he flew at your throat. I suppose he thought we were going to swipe his dinner, but no matter what time of day it was he always reacted the same. Once he ripped my brother up so badly we had to have him put away. My brother. Not the dog. Maybe Mother *was* a gypsy.

My father was more on the down-to-earth side. He worked as a cable engineer. I never found out what a cable engineer was, and still don't know. He had something to do with the Atlantic cables, and every once in a while the company packed him off to Newfoundland or the Azores, and once to Midway. What the hell *Midway* had to do with the *Atlantic* cables is anybody's guess, but while he was there (it was during World War I), a German raiding party took over the island, wrecked the cable station and took off again with a warning to Dad and a few others not to call the police for ten minutes.

CHAPTER 2

Summertime and The Livin' Is Ridiculous

ONE SUMMER, when they could afford it, my parents sent me to camp. The camp was located in the foothills of the foothills of the Catskills. The camp was called Camp Moc-a-doc, which was an Indian name, they told us. I now have seven huge books on the American Indian, and Moc-a-doc has no meaning at all. The camp was owned by an outdoor what-makes-Sammy-run type of guy who insisted we all call him "Uncle Al." I found out later that his name was Joe, but he thought "Uncle Al" sounded friendlier. Nevertheless, we Moc-a-docers still called him Uncle Fart. Due to some misalignment of his intestinal tubes, this was very appropriate. He could have serviced a Zeppelin single-handed.

Camp Moc-a-doc was on the shores of beautiful Lake Sacawawa, another old Indian name, and according to the legend, the lake was called Sacawawa because an Indian named Sacawawa had once drowned in it. And as he was drowning, he had called to his friend on the shore, "Sacawawa! Sacawawa!" By the time his friend had run to the nearest Indian village to ask the chief what "Sacawawa" meant, the drowning Indian had drowned. I looked up "Sacawawa" in one of my seven books on the American Indian and it means "Moc-a-doc."

When you first arrived at Camp Moc-a-doc, you were assigned to a tent, one that Uncle Fart had picked up from a war surplus store. Our tent was called "Teepee-in-Pines." We called it Andersonville.

The second thing they did when you arrived was give you an Indian name. I was in a tent with Sitting Bull Needlebaum, Running Water O'Rourke, Standing Bear Graziano, and Tree Top Tall Schwartz.

Next, you were put on a team. Even if you couldn't play softball, tennis or ping pong, or ride or swim or jump or *anything*, you were still assigned to a team. Because if you were not on a team, you wouldn't get your name in the camp paper, and if you didn't get your name in the camp paper, how would the folks back home know that you were having a wonderful time at Camp Moc-a-doc? *I* was on a team. I was on the Conquerors. We played softball. We also used a soft bat. They wouldn't trust us with anything else, and we *never* won a game with *anybody*. But at the end of the season we all got big "C's" to put on the front of what was left of our sweaters. We also got a blue ribbon which had in gold lettering "Camp Moc-a-doc First," which I thought just about reached the peak, noncommittal-wise. According to my old Year Book, everybody in camp got a blue ribbon for something. Herbie Windham got a blue ribbon for making his bed in the record time of one hour and twenty-three minutes. Joey Henshow got a blue ribbon for helping him. Roger Pincus got a blue ribbon for *not* helping him. Gary Kaskel got a blue ribbon for washing his hands. He also got another blue ribbon for *drying* them (on a towel). Rupert Lomm got a blue ribbon for blowing "Taps" on his bugle every morning, and Maxie Trimpton got a blue ribbon for leaving *his* bugle home. One kid, who shall be nameless, got a blue ribbon because he wore a pony tail. He was the camp's camp. Anyway, you can see the psychology that Uncle Fart was using: nobody ever left Camp Moc-a-doc a loser.

The counselors at Camp Moc-a-doc were a pretty nice bunch. I think we had the best though. His name was Lou Bond, and he had an endless supply of dirty jokes and cigarettes. Some of the jokes we didn't quite understand (a nine-year-old kid doesn't dig *everything*), but he smoked Camels, which he sold us, one at a time, so at the end of the season we nominated him for "Counselor-of-the-Year," but he lost out to Johnny Wick. Johnny was a little more enterprising: he had French postcards and sold *cigars*.

The food at Camp Moc-a-doc showed marked improvement on the days the mothers and fathers came up to visit the inmates. We had steak instead of beans for lunch, and ice cream instead of jello. Two of the rainiest Saturdays of the season were set aside for parents' visiting days. This, of course, meant that most of the activity had to be confined to the "Rec" hall, where we were supposed to show Mother and Dad the progress we had been making at camp. My mother and dad were *very* impressed with the way I could tie my shoelaces with one hand. My other hand was covered with bandages from a how-to-tell-poison-ivy-from-poison-oak lesson. Some of the kids who were adept at "Arts and Crafts" had hand-painted ceramic ashtrays to show their parents. These always made a big impression. The paint was made from an old Indian formula, and never dried. Later in the afternoon, after a few Tarzan movies with Eddie Polo, everybody was dying for a cigarette—especially the kids, so we all moved outside—rain or no. Actually, we moved outside because a swimming meet was next on the agenda. This was especially interesting for the parents, because instead of getting a wire or a phone call, they could actually *watch* little Herbie drown.

The day after visiting day was always beautiful and sunny and warm and a lot more relaxed. Uncle Fart put away his "King of the Royal Mounties" outfit and went back to his sweatshirt and blue jeans, and we kids spent the day ducking the counselors, who, after counting the take from the kitty which was set up for donations from grateful parents, were in no mood to play big brother to anyone.

Camp Moc-a-doc is no more, but looking back through the rosy glow of a foggy memory it wasn't so bad. I remember the last night in camp. We were all sitting around the campfire. There was an enormous moon coming up behind the pine trees. We had been singing all the old camping songs, and had just finished the last few bars of "Home on the Range," when Alfy Gruner, apparently carried away by all this nostalgia, suddenly stood up and to the melody of the Cornell Alma Mater, sang:

21

"Far above Sacawawa's waters
On this night when we must part,
We'll never forget Camp Moc-a-doc
And dear old Uncle Fart."

CHAPTER 3

Rudy Vallee Is A Capitalist

ALL THE TIME I was going to Lynbrook High I had been studying the drums. I used to play in the school orchestra, and I was pretty good, especially when they played "Onward Christian Soldiers." *That*, at least, had a beat. One afternoon, while hanging around the corner of 49th Street and Broadway with my drums, trying to look like a professional musician (49th and Broadway was where they used to loiter), some guy offered me a job with a name band.

It was a name that nobody had ever heard of, but I was in heaven. One of the first jobs we had was at Madison Square Garden, playing for a dance marathon. In those days every drummer had to be a singer, too, so I sang from the bandstand, which was in the center of the Garden, with a megaphone. I doubt if more than three people heard me, and, with that megaphone and the bad lighting, the people who saw me probably thought I was just a Ubangi—trying to mix. My best number was "Over There," a war song. I was a little late with this item, but I thought maybe I could stir up a little something. Maybe only a gang rumble. Anyway, I was in show business and I was happy. That is, until I heard that Rudy Vallee, who also sang with a megaphone, was getting $19,950 more a week than I was. So I switched to boxing. I was still going to school, so it took me quite a long time to get back to Madison Square Garden in that sweaty racket, but I finally made it. I fought a four-round "prelim" for fifty dollars. Rudy Vallee was *still* making $19,950 more a week than I was. But *I* had a broken nose.

By this time, I was quite a celebrity in Lynbrook. I got my name in *The New Era,* which was Lynbrook's leading (and only) newspaper; and at "the Greek's" I had a drink named after me—the "Crickard Special"—which was orange juice loaded with maraschino cherries and served in a dirty glass (that wasn't part of the "special"—that was part of the Greek's). Incidentally, "Crickard" is my legal name, and there are very few Crickards. I've looked in phone books around the country and have only found this name in New York, Washington, D.C., Chicago and Glendale, California. I've never discovered the reason for so few Crickards. Either they're slow breeders or they just have more unlisted phone numbers.

Life in Lynbrook was very simple. For one thing, we had no color problem. Mainly, I suppose, because we were all *plaid.* We did have a local branch of the Ku Klux Klan, but they were sort of a homey bunch. Every time they'd burn a cross in somebody's front yard, they'd roast a few marshmallows and distribute them to the neighborhood kiddies.

And in Lynbrook, there was no prejudice against minority groups. None at all. They were much better armed. I remember only one instance of any kind of prejudice. Mr. Purdy, who lived in a one-room shack near the swamps, hated Girl Scout cookies, and this was years before they even *had* Girl Scout cookies, but Mr. Purdy said he had a feeling they were coming, and he just wanted to be ready. Every high school senior class puts on a class play, and Lynbrook High was no different. Of course, nowadays they put on *South Pacific* and *A Streetcar Named Desire* and *Irma La Douce* and stuff like that, but in *my* day we had to be content with *The Pirate's Daughter*, *Cherry Blossoms of the Emperor* which, incidentally, is a Greek situation-tragedy, and *Sandra of the Yukon* (an *Alaskan* situation-tragedy).

The Lynbrook High School play was called *The Pirate's Daughter* and it was all about a pirate who had a daughter. Surprised? Anyway, the action of the play took place in Holland. I've forgotten whether the pirate was Dutch, or he was just visiting or maybe he was stealing tulips. I've forgotten. All I remember actually was that in the play I sang a song called: "I'm Just a Butterfly That's Caught in the Rain." My memory is a little hazy about the whole thing. I don't remember whether I was the *pirate* or the daughter. But it was kind of a strange song for a pirate to sing, and we had *girls* in the senior class, so I couldn't have been playing the daughter—although thinking back about the girls at Lynbrook High, maybe I *did* play the daughter. Nevertheless, I had one line in the play, just one line. I was supposed to say: "Happy Birthday, Burgomaster" to the Burgomaster, but for some strange reason I said: "Good Morning, Burgomaster." The kid playing the Burgomaster, who, incidentally, was the smartest kid in the whole school, replied, "Thank you." I'm sorry now that I didn't say: "Burgomaster, *you* are a son of a bitch." I'm sure he still would have said: "Thank you."

CHAPTER 4

Guest Star At A Massacre

In 1928 my father picked up some lung trouble long before it was the smart thing, and he and my mother sold the Lynbrook house and moved to California. They moved to a charming little health resort called Banning, which is familiar to every Hollywoodite as the town where you get arrested for speeding on the way to Palm Springs. My brother was still at Harvard, and I was still a bum. I now lived in a cubicle in a shabby brownstone on West 70th Street in New York. I think it must have been the most depressing room in all of Manhattan. Iron bed. Bathroom down the hall. A three-watt bulb hanging from the ceiling, and foghorns from the Hudson going all night long. There were no beams in the ceiling to throw a rope over or I think that would have been it: "Landlady Finds Transient Hanging in Room, Fifteen Cents Sewn to Underwear."

Before I had saved enough money for a rope (I belonged to a Christmas Club), I seriously took up boxing, or the manly art of self-defense, as it was known (everywhere except in the boxing business).

Mr. Heckheimer, a wealthy Lynbrook resident, decided that I was going to be the next heavyweight champion of the world. I only weighed about a hundred and sixty, but Mr. Heckheimer had divine faith. I had had lots of amateur experience as a boxer, from a flyweight to a middleweight, in the local clubs around Long Island, and had picked up quite a few gold (?) watches, but what I needed now was professional guidance and handling. Mr. Heckheimer sent me to Gus Wilson's training camp at Orangeburg, New York.

Wilson's camp was very famous in those days, as was Wilson himself. He was a Frenchman, and had trained Georges Carpentier for his bout with Dempsey. Carpentier, the "Orchid Man," hadn't done too well with Dempsey, but he made Gus famous. Life at Wilson's training camp was monotonous. Every morning before breakfast there was roadwork. Marty Gallagher, a pretty good heavyweight from Washington, D.C., and I did roadwork together. Marty was a very likeable and easygoing guy, and I was no firebrand either, so our roadwork left much to be desired. Sometimes we would just run around a bend in the road, out of Gus's sight, then sit down under a tree, and after enough time had elapsed to equal about five or six miles of roadwork, we'd go puffing back to camp. Naturally, we were only kidding ourselves when we goofed off, because without a lot of roadwork a boxer has no legs, and a boxer with no legs is no good. Suppose you wanna run a little in the ring?

Gus Wilson was an excellent trainer, but he had a disconcerting habit of throwing punches at you whenever he felt like it and when you were off guard. This could happen as you were walking by him in the hall, or getting up from the dinner table, or just as you were buttoning your fly in the john. This was supposed to teach you to protect yourself at all times. And it did. After a while, and a short while too, you learned to pick off Gus's punches with your shoulders or elbows or hands almost with reflex action.

Gus put me into the capable hands of a very wily old Negro fighter who went under the name of the "Jamaica Kid." He knew every trick of the boxing business and, although he was nearly blind by this time, he was very difficult to hit, but he could hit me almost whenever he felt like it. I learned a lot from the Jamaica Kid, even though he was a little hard to understand at times, because as he was teaching me to slip and roll and counterpunch, he would suddenly come out with: ". . . and the good Lord said unto him . . . always cover with your chin . . . you throw a left . . . your right covers your chin . . . you throw a right . . . your left covers your chin . . . it is more blessed to give than receive. . . ." I think the Kid had a point here with this last, especially in boxing, but actually his mind was a little befuddled from all the years of getting his head pounded, and he used to mix the Marquis of Queensberry with the Golden Rule quite frequently. He was a little hard to follow at times, but I understood enough to become a pretty good boxer.

The last time I saw the Jamaica Kid was quite a few years

later. He was standing outside the St. Nicholas arena in New York on fight night. He had a tin cup and some pencils. I put some money in his cup but I didn't speak to him. I knew he wouldn't remember me, because even at the camp he wouldn't remember me from one day to the next. With him I was always the "new boy."

There were quite a few celebrated boxers at the camp in the three months I was there: Jack Sharkey, just before he became heavyweight champion by knocking out Max Schmeling; Jackie "Kid" Berg, lightweight champion of Britain; and Vittorio Campolo (from Argentina), who was six feet eight inches tall, and a real berserker. Campolo was supposed to be the successor to Luis Angel Firpo, his countryman, who came within inches of the heavyweight crown by knocking Jack Dempsey out of the ring a few years before. I say he was a real berserker because when he boxed he looked like he was fighting a forest fire, and he didn't care if he hit you in the knee—if it did damage. Poor Vittorio, after a couple of disasters in the ring he went back to Buenos Aires and became a hat designer.

Sundays at Gus Wilson's training camp was sort of visitors' day. One Sunday, among others, Jack Johnson, who had been the world's champion from 1908 to 1915, arrived on the scene. He was one of the greatest boxers of all times, and he demonstrated this by getting into the ring and making pencil marks around his feet on the canvas. Then he invited anybody who would, to hit him, either in the body or in the head. He wouldn't punch back. Almost every boxer in the camp tried, and nobody, including Sharkey, could hit him. Johnson just stood in his marks, ducking and weaving and moving his head ever so slightly. I've never seen anything like this before or since. He was like a big black cat covered with grease. I don't know how old he was at the time, but he must have been at least sixty, and he made all of us young cats look like kittens.

Another Sunday, Rudy Vallee, the Vagabond Lover, visited the camp, and made the mistake of taking off his clothes and posing in boxing shorts for the photographers, and he really proved by this picture, which was circulated throughout the world, that he was a lover and not a fighter. I still have a copy of the picture, and every time I look at it I'm astounded all over again. Underneath Rudy's Kollege Kut Klothes, there had been no body at all. Just a few coat hangers soldered together.

I got to be quite a big boy during my stay with Gus. I was the only one at the camp who got three meals a day. Every one else only got two. Of course they were enormous meals. They *had* to be for some of the gorillas we had there. But I was trying to put on weight, so I got three *enormous* meals a day, plus ice cream in between meals. And in between meals and ice cream and roadwork and training periods, I dug holes, filled wheelbarrows with the dirt, wheeled the wheelbarrow a few hundred feet, dumped it, then dug another hole and repeated the whole procedure all over again. I looked like an apprentice idiot, if you were watching me closely, but what I was doing (according to Gus) was building up my back muscles and, at the same time, my arm strength.

When I got to weigh about 165 or 170, Gus decided I was ready for my moment of truth. It happened at a place called Newburgh, a town on the Hudson River. Not that it matters where it happened. Like Waterloo, it was just a town. Actually, in defense of my prowess as a (for the first time) professional boxer, I must say that fate took a large part in this debilitating debacle. In the first place, when I arrived in Newburgh, at the local fight club, with most everybody from Gus's to cheer me on—and up—I found out that the guy I was supposed to box—"a Newburgh boy and not too tough"—had either taken sick or a run-out powder, so in order not to disappoint the local sadists, they matched me with another boy they said I "could take care of, so don't worry." Well, it didn't work out quite that way. Oh, I could have *taken care* of him all right—if I'd had a Colt forty-five, or a Samurai sword, or a poison ring or something—but with just my fists and six-ounce gloves I didn't do so well. He knocked me down twice in each of the first five rounds. In the sixth round he knocked me down three times. This was his best round. Between rounds I had a little difficulty in finding my corner, and after I found it I was kinda sorry; *everybody* from camp had some *advice* for me, none of which I could follow. I *couldn't* stay out of his way, because they wouldn't let me go back to the dressing room. I *couldn't* crowd him (to shorten up his punches), because he had eight-foot arms. I *couldn't* bring his guard down to get a crack at his chin, because he not only had eight-foot arms—he had *four* of them. Despite all the pleas from the boys to "go out there and get him for Old Gus!" I settled for just going out there. That was about all I could do. He won a unanimous decision. Even *I* voted for him.

CHAPTER 5

Virginia Dare and My First Flying Lesson

AFTER A FEW MORE attempts in the ring I was saved by a job with another orchestra, Al Vann's. Mr. Vann's chief claims to fame were that he had once written the music to Walter Winchell's lyrics for the song "Things I Never Knew Till Now," and he was married to the Ritz brothers' sister. She didn't look like them, which I thought was good taste. We opened at the old Hippodrome Theatre and were instantaneously adequate, as one critic put it. I played the drums and sang "It's a Treat to Beat Your Feet in the Mississippi Mud" with a trio.

The arrangement we stole in toto from Paul Whiteman's Rhythm Boys (Harry Barris, Bing Crosby and Al Rinker). Actually, we didn't do a bad job, and a week later we were booked at the Poli Theatre in Norwalk, Connecticut, then the Tilyou Theatre in Coney Island, and the Palace Theatre

33

in Bangor, Maine. We were "going places," everybody told us, and they were right. After that we played the Palace Theatre in Bayonne, New Jersey, the Palace Theatre in Drummondville, Quebec, and the Palace Theatre in Butte, Montana. In Butte, I got drunk for the first time in my life. This was still during prohibition days, and a couple of us punks wanted to get drunk, so we went to a recommended speakeasy where, seeing how young we were, they sold us a bottle of Virginia Dare wine-tonic, which, of course, we had no reason to believe wasn't real "Dago red," which is what we wanted. We went back to our hotel and had a few slugs of this thickly sweet tonic, which contains about 3 per cent alcohol, and was sold almost anywhere legally as a tonic for run-down people. Alcoholic run-down people, I presume. Anyway, it didn't take us long to catch on that we had been sold slop, so we went back to the speak and asked for something with a little more zip. The bent-nose boy who let us in told us to wait a minute, that he'd fix us right up. He did. To the half-consumed bottle of Virginia Dare he added a pint of moonshine rye whiskey, saying "That oughta do it."

Well, it did it all right. For some reason, I woke up on the stage of the Palace Theatre about six a.m. the next morning, stretched out on a couch. I hadn't the slightest idea where I was. The couch was part of a living room set used by another act on the bill and looked like part of a hotel room. There was a bare work light burning in the middle of the stage, and gradually I became aware of someone moving around down in the orchestra seats. Finally, I realized where I was, and the person down in the orchestra was the cleaning woman. I doubted very much whether I

34

could get up by myself, so I called to her. This was a mistake. She hadn't been aware of me until I called, so she panicked and let go with a blood-curdling scream. At that same moment two wild beasts she had with her (who later turned out to be two lovable Pekinese dogs) flew up the stairs at the side of the stage and came right at me. I got up without assistance and raced (after a fashion) for the back door. The two dogs were much faster and to this day I still carry an ankle full of Pekinese teeth marks. That cured me. I've never been able to drink a Pekinese since.

After our musical tour of the culture-hungry countryside, where, after we finished, "silence, like a poultice, came to heal the blows of sound," to quote another critic, Al Vann and his orchestra returned to New York, ready to open at the *New York* Palace Theatre. *We* were ready but *they* weren't. This was a terrible blow to me, so I quit being a vaudeville star and became a caddy. One week and three hundred and fifty-two lost balls later, the caddy master suggested I go back to being a vaudeville star. This was impossible, so I decided to become an airplane stunt flyer. I don't know how I got this insane idea, because I was terrified of height and speed.

The only flyer I knew at this time was a man on the Long Beach Road who, on weekends, took people up in his plane for a dollar a minute, a pretty good price. He had been or was a famous stunt flyer, and although I don't remember *his* name, the plane was called the "Bluebird." It was a biplane and painted blue, and was held together with St. Christopher medals. He agreed to teach me to fly for ten dollars per half hour, in his spare time. My first lesson was my last. The Bluebird, which featured an open cockpit, took off from its cow pasture air strip, and headed north over the swamps of East Rockaway and into a flock of ducks who had also just taken off and were heading south. The cockpit was suddenly full of feathers, and the whole thing was just like a Keystone Comedy, except that the right wing strut had collapsed from the duck impact and the upper and lower wings were flapping merrily in the breeze. This was one stunt I hadn't counted on learning, not the first day anyway. I sat there paralyzed—in my damp shorts. But not for long. Somewhere between "Our Father who . . ." and ". . . art in Heaven" we smacked into the swamp, nose first. The Bluebird was a mess, but we were okay. Climbing down into the soft ooze of the swamp, I'm not sure, but I thought I heard a mushrat titter.

After this abortive attempt to become King of the Jungle overnight, by pulling some strings I got a job as an office boy in the office of a friend of mine. Actually, I was *more* than just an *office* boy; I was a *messenger* boy, too. One of my chores was to take large sums of money from New York over to a warehouse in Long Island City, and give the money to a group who seemed to be just hanging around the warehouse. This I did every week or so. The group at the warehouse acted very jittery every time I opened the door and walked in (the door was never locked), so I remarked about it one day. When I got back to the office, my boss asked me what the hell was I tryna do—scare them guys to death? I said, "No." And he said, "No more remarks when you go over there"; and I said, "Okay"; and that was that. Then one day I went to the warehouse with a fist full of large bills in my hot little briefcase, and found the place crawling with cops. Immediately, they surrounded me and said, "Whaddya got in the briefcase?" And I said, "Money." They said, "Let's see it," and when I showed it to them, they promptly confiscated it. Then they said, "Do you know what's in them bales?" And I said, "No." Then they said, "*Look*," ripping the paper off one of the bales. It looked like red rope. But when I said, "Gee, red rope," they said, "Red rope, hell, that's raw silk," and when I said, "So what?" they said, "*So what*, it's stolen!" Then I said, "Oh." After questioning me for a few hours, they figured I was too dumb for the raw silk hijacking business, so they let me go. I don't know what happened to my boss or the nervous group at the warehouse. I know what happened to me. I left the next day for California—by rocket.

CHAPTER 6

Hollywood and Chicago, or *From Chorus Boy To Fan Dancer in Ten Short Years*

THE NIGHT I ARRIVED in Hollywood was the night they premiered the great war picture *Hell's Angels*. I was *not* invited, but I *went* anyway. I stood outside Grauman's Chinese Theatre with thousands of other yokels, and thought it was the most fabulous sight I had ever seen. Planes were strafing the crowd. Soldiers were shooting down autograph hounds who got too close to the stars, and everybody screamed and swooned every time Loretta Young pulled up in front of the theatre in a golden pumpkin drawn by five thousand white mice. This, I thought, was *living! Really* living!

With the help of Douglas Fairbanks, Senior, a stock company friend of my mother's, I didn't get a job in the movies. But I *did* get a job in a little speakeasy type of place called Harry O'Day's, in Culver City, where I was a drummer, for dancing, and a table singer, for entertainment. Table singing wasn't the most pleasant way in the world of earning a buck. You had to have the guts of General Patton and the hide of Tony Galento, plus the smile of Liberace. I had all three, out of necessity. Table singing was just that. You went over to a table, sang a song, then asked: "Well, folks, what would you like to hear?" Most of the time, if it was a table for two, the guy was a helluva lot more interested in hearing "Yes" from his cuddly girl friend than "Tea for Two" from a brash stranger, so you'd usually pick up quite a few bucks to "Get lost!" Occasionally though, you'd come across a music lover who wanted to hear everything from "Melancholy Baby" to "Rock of Ages" (not much of a beat to this last one), but music lovers, while appreciative, were not too flush. To them, twenty-five cents a song was the limit. At that price, you not only had to sing your little heart out to make the rent, but it kept you from annoying your wealthy "Get lost!" customers.

One night, Bing Crosby, then at the Ambassador Hotel's Coconut Grove, was unceremoniously asked to find another job because, suddenly and quite unexpectedly during the second chorus of "Tiptoe Through the Tulips," he tossed his cookies too close to some totally unprepared tippy-toeing tourist. The very next night, with the confidence of a bomb thrower at an Algerian picnic, I strode back of the bandstand at the Grove and *told*, not *asked*, the bandleader, Jimmy

Grier, that I wanted to sing. He said, "What song?" And I said, "I'll Be Glad When You're Dead, You Rascal You." He said, "Okay." I sang and I got the job. Leonard Goldstein, later a producer in the movies but then handling things at the Grove, gave me a contract that same night. I was a smash. One month later I was playing the drums and table singing in a dump in Oxnard, California, for one dollar a night, room and board, and I had to sleep in a single bed with a three-hundred-pound piano player, who was not only a lousy piano player, but a male. I don't know what happened to *me* at the Coconut Grove. *I* didn't toss *my* cookies.

A couple of years later when I met Cliff Arquette, who has now become famous by playing Charlie Weaver, a dirty old man, on the Paar show, he was playing the part of Aunt Addie, a dirty old lady, on a local Hollywood radio show. He and I and a very funny guy, Red Corcoran, teamed up and became alternately "The Three Ex-Rhythm Boys" and "The Three Public Enemies." We worked on a show called "The Franco Hi-Jinks," which had nothing to do with Fun-in-a-Dictator's-Bedroom. Franco was the name of a bakery. Cliff, Red and I didn't make much money, but we gained confidence. Especially me. After a couple of months on the Hi-Jinks show, I drove to San Francisco and walked into a big benefit being held at a huge auditorium there. I used the Coconut Grove technique: I walked up to the bandleader, Phil Harris, and said I wanted to sing. He said, "What song?" and I said, "I'll Be Glad When You're Dead, You Rascal You." He said, "Okay," and with the backing of seventy-five musicians (I said it was a benefit), I sang. Everything worked perfectly. I got a job at a San Francisco radio station, KFRC. The show was the Blue Monday Jamboree, which made everything fine. My Hollywood show was on Fridays, so all I had to do was drive back and forth between San Francisco and Hollywood, over the *Old* Ridge Route in an open car— and driving the *Old* Ridge Route in any kind of car was the equivalent of flying the Hump with feathers glued to your wrists. But I made it, even though sometimes I arrived in Hollywood with my left hand frozen to my crotch, where I had placed it in case of warmth.

Nevertheless, things were looking up. I also got a job dancing in the chorus of *Whoopee*, a technicolor movie starring Eddie Cantor. It was a Western and we were all cowboys, and the first thing I did on the first day's shooting was to dance backwards and sink the rowel of one of my spurs into Lucille Ball's instep. Not that anybody cared. Except maybe Lucille. She was just a showgirl then. Little did any of us know that someday she would wind up owning 50 per cent of a bongo player.

Betty Grable was also in *Whoopee*. She was about fourteen years old at the time, but built like the Alamo. Like somebody said, "She looked like she'd been taking knocker pills since she was three."

I worked as a chorus boy in quite a few Hollywood musicals. Not that I was much of a dancer. Practically the only requirement then was that you be tall, have hair and tap shoes. Everything was tap! tap! tap! With the invention of the sneaker, tap dancing died out completely, and so did chorus boys in Hollywood. Most of them became chorus girls.

There was an enormous roadhouse in Culver City, called the Cotton Club, and it was run by a very suave individual by the name of Frank Sebastian. He was really an old smoothie. No matter what night of the week it was or what season (Lent included), there were always hundreds of cars parked around the place, giving the impression, when you drove by, that the place was jammed. However, in the daytime, when the place wasn't even open, the parking lot was still crowded. Sebastian used to buy wrecked cars and stash them all over to give the capacity business impression, but that's Culver City for you. All tinsel and make-believe.

I worked at the Cotton Club, doing a sort of singing, mixed with comedy, act. Lots of movie stars used to come in (they had to park in back of the wrecked cars), and one night I was "discovered" by Buddy Rogers and Mary Pickford, and the next thing I knew I was a band clown and singer with Buddy in Chicago. The World's Fair was on and we played at the Sherman Hotel's College Inn until about ten every evening; then we jumped into a cabin cruiser and sailed over to the fair grounds to finish out the night at the Pabst Blue Ribbon Casino. It was a ball. The night Sally Rand was arrested for lewdity, I rolled up my pants, took two paper fans, walked out on the floor and did my version of her dance (which I had never seen). Timeliness made it a howler, and although Buddy inwardly cringed at every performance, I kept it in and it became almost as famous as Sally's.

During the Chicago Fair I was introduced to Will Rogers, Tyrone Power, Tony Martin, marijuana and a nymphomaniac. Will Rogers was a friendly man, full of homely sick humor. Tyrone Power was working in a World's Fair exhibit that showed the rubes how movies were made.

Tony Martin was a saxophone player in a hotel band, using the stage name "Al Morris." Marijuana was cute but boring. The nymphomaniac was a lot friendlier than Will Rogers.

Chicago made the big mistake of holding the Fair over for a second year, and *we* made the big mistake of coming *back* the second time. The Pabst Casino had more rats than customers. Toward the end of the second season, the customers demanded equal rights, the rats started picketing, and overnight the magic of it all was gone. And so were we.

CHAPTER 7

New Year's Eve In, I Think, Buffalo

TRAVELLING WITH A ROAD BAND can be great fun if you have no manners, morals or nose. In less than a week a bus full of musicians can smell like a truckload of llamas who haven't been well, on a hot day in Guatamala.

With Buddy Rogers (and his band), I saw a helluva lot of country by bus, and I think it was during this period I picked up my distrust of anybody else's driving. We travelled by chartered bus, and the chartered driver kept the same hours that we did. Consequently, there was quite a lot of what I called "the falling asleep at the wheel" bit, which, during the five-hundred-mile jumps between jobs, kept nobody awake except me. I watched every turn and bend, and half of the musicians in this country today are alive only because of me. I *never* slept. ". . . leave the driving to *us!*" Horse apples!

One night during a dance in Pismo Beach, California, some wise punk squirted Buddy with a seltzer bottle, and I've never seen anybody move so fast. Buddy dove from the bandstand and in three seconds flat was having a jolly time strangling the guy to death and at the same time beating his head against the dance floor. We were playing a rhumba, and I've got to give Buddy credit—he was right on the beat—albeit for the first time.

Actually, Buddy Rogers was a very talented man. At the period when he was "America's Boyfriend," he was a hotter star than any we have today. During a personal appearance engagement at New York's Paramount Theatre, he had to maintain suites in five different hotels to keep the fans guessing, or else he never would have reached home alive. When he was hot, he made Rudolph Valentino look like Marvin Krine. Buddy Rogers was really the Wildroot Charlie of the Thwarted Thirties. Besides being almost a pretty boy, he was very talented. He could play "Sugar Blues" on the trumpet, "Blue Room" on the clarinet, "Liebestraum" on the trombone, and "Twelfth Street Rag" on *everything*. He could also sing a little ("It's Only a Paper Moon" and *Faust*). He could type like a court stenographer, and finger talk to the deaf and dumb because in his home town of Olathe, Kansas, there was a large deaf and dumb institute which consisted of more than half the population, so if you wanted to get through to 'em you had to talk their language, so to speak—or is it, so to thumb?

I don't think Buddy ever quite understood me, or really wanted to. I'll have to admit giving him a few headaches. One New Year's Eve we were playing in Shea's Buffalo, a theatre in Buffalo, New York. I guess it *had* to be. But, anyway, we had a midnight show to do, so between the last show, which ended about ten-thirty, and midnight, Gene Krupa, Buddy's drummer at that time, and Toots Mondello, the great reed man, and myself repaired to my room to have a few blasts. We did, and we all felt wonderful. We walked back to the theatre. It was the coldest night they'd had in Buffalo for sixty years, as it always *is* in Buffalo, but it was very bracing after the amount of booze we'd put away. Everything was fine until those hot lights hit us. I don't remember much about how Gene and Toots felt. All I know is that during my act in which I used a football referee's whistle during a song "You've Gotta Be a Football Hero to Get Along with the Beautiful Girls," some joker in the first row started to blow a fish-horn at me, so I stopped whatever I was doing to blow my referee's whistle back at him. Well, that was the act for the Gala New Year's Eve Show at Shea's Buffalo, the Theatre for Family Entertainment—a drunk in the first row blowing a fish-horn and a drunk on the stage blowing a referee's whistle back at him, for a good *fifteen minutes!* Finally, they lowered the asbestos curtain hoping they'd hit me, and that was the end of the Gala New Year's Eve Shows at Shea's Buffalo—forever. And the end of me with Buddy Rogers.

CHAPTER 8

Thirteen Guys Named Jesus

MY NEXT ENGAGEMENT, after a non-tearful farewell to Buddy Rogers, was playing drums with a Cuban rhumba band, Carlos Molina's. We played in the Blossom Room at the Hollywood Roosevelt Hotel. We might just as well have been playing in the Lily Room at Forest Lawn. We had only three customers every night: Charlie Chaplin and Paulette Goddard, who came in to dance with each other, and Ferdinand Gottschalk, an old character actor, who came in to eat his dinner, alone. None of the three ever made a sound of appreciation or even glanced in our direction. It was like playing for the last three people on earth, and the whole thing was happening under water.

New Year's Eve (here we go again) was different at the Blossom Room. Plus Charlie and Paulette and Ferdinand, we had people. Lots and lots of people, and they were all loaded. I was very square in those days, so I got loaded, too. Suddenly, I found myself at the Hollywood police station, sitting on a stool next to the desk sergeant. It seems that I had thrown a salt shaker through a huge plate glass mirror in the hotel lobby (after seeing my reflection). I know now why I did it. I hated the little red jackets we had to wear in the band, and my reflection plus a few shots of straight alcohol had transformed me from Jane to Tarzan. I sat next to the desk sergeant all night, and in the morning the manager of the hotel came and got me, and took me home. I didn't get fired this time. I had to pay for the mirror first. Consequently, I was the Blossom Room's permanent drummer. No matter whose band was playing there (and there were quite a few), Jack, the salt-shaker-thrower, was on the skins. Eventually, the mirror was paid for and I was dropped like a hot rock. But I'll always remember those Blossom Room days and the Carlos Molina group, mainly because there were thirteen guys in the band named "Jesus." Those Cubans don't take any chances, do they?

CHAPTER 9

A Visit To The Mother Country

In 1938, all hell was breaking out in Europe. I was playing in variety in England, and for all I knew or cared, Hitler and Mussolini were a dance team. I was a pretty good stand-up comedian by this time. A stand-up comedian is somebody who can stand up and be a comedian, and I could do a little of both, so some demented English booking agent, who had seen me in Newark (N.J.), had booked me on a tour of England. My first date, in February, was in Liverpool. I arrived in Liverpool on a Saturday night by clipper (the kind with sails, not wings), and checked in at the Stork Hotel, which I had understood to be the best hotel in Liverpool. It *could* be, but the room I had was the Liverpool version of the Black Hole of Calcutta, plus a few English refinements like a twenty-watt bulb for feeling.

If you wanted to feel where the bed was, you lit the light. And a shilling gas meter for heat (which was mailed to you in a plain wrapper). That first night I slept under three blankets, which had been dipped in brine in case of dryness, and awoke the next morning ready for a Sunday in Liverpool. I discovered in no time at all that I wasn't *quite* ready. Sunday in Liverpool is like Sunday nowhere else on earth. In the first place, if you're a stranger, rain is arranged. But not just ordinary rain that pitter-patters and puddles. This rain is all the monsoon seasons that ever happened anywhere on earth since time began, and this all happens in one day—Sunday in Liverpool. There are no people on the streets. Just shipwrecks. You can't buy a drink or a cigarette or a candy bar or sandwich. Opium you can buy. Not legally, of course, but Sundays in Liverpool, the Narcotics Squad has a holiday. I don't know *how* they spend it, but smoking opium—if they're *smart*.

The next night I opened at the Shakespeare Theatre, which is a variety house. I had a good spot on the bill, and although I got heckled from the gallery when I first walked out on the stage, I managed to say just the right thing back, got a big round of applause for saying it, then proceeded to get a lot of laughs from my act, wound up with the song "Mamma Don't Allow" and walked off, as they say in the trade papers, to "good mitting." I was very relieved, because up until twenty years before, this very same theatre used to have a steel netting rigged up in front of the gallery, which was usually filled with shipyard workers (from across the river) who had a habit of pelting the actors with nuts, bolts and rivets when they didn't quite agree with *your* idea of what should entertain *them*. The net was gone now, but the same bunch from across the river were still patrons of the Shakespeare.

Incidentally, across the river (the Mersey) is the town of Birkenhead, and it was here that variety, or vaudeville, first came into being. Harry Lauder was one of the first performers at that theatre. He was such a big hit with the Birkenheadians that the management prevailed upon him to sign a lifetime contract, at three pounds a week, for one week every year. To Lauder, who in those days was a nobody, this looked like a pretty good deal, but as the years passed and he became famous and could demand almost any price and get it, he still had to play in Birkenhead for three pounds per week. This outraged Lauder, who was a slow man with a shilling, but the stubborn management of the Birkenhead Theatre would never release him from this lifetime obligation.

I never met Harry Lauder, but I did play on the bill a few times with another great English favorite, Will Fyffe. Fyffe was a character comedian, and he used to play several different characters during his thirty-minute turn. What amazed me was that he used to change his clothes and character make-up *offstage*, while the orchestra simply played a few tunes. Nothing happened *onstage* at all, and some of Fyffe's changes used to take three or four minutes. It seems that in England, if they like you, they'll wait for you. Of course, in America, if they *don't* like you, they'll wait for you. In a more secluded spot, naturally.

I did very well in England, but I flopped miserably in Scotland. A little Scottish comic on the same bill was a smash. He wore kilts, told Scottish jokes and played the bagpipes for a finish; he had the audience tearing up the seats.

Then I walked *on* to a stony silence, and walked *off* to a stony silence, and sandwiched in between those two stony silences was a long stretch of absolute quiet. I'm quite sure they liked my act, but they suspected that I was English, and no English comic *ever* got a laugh in Scotland. They're still sore about Mary.

My undoing (and I was always being undone, it seemed) in England was a theatre manager in Coventry. He insisted that I do my act in the number two spot, which meant that I would go on right after the opening trick bike-riding act. I insisted that I had never, since I'd been in England, had anything but a headline spot—right before the interval (intermission) or the second act *after* the interval. The theatre manager still insisted, and so did I. As a consequence I didn't go on at all, and I was through, so far as variety in England was concerned. Theatre managers stick together over there, and by my stubbornness in Coventry I had blackballed myself from appearing anywhere else. So I went back to London, had a few blasts, saw a beautiful Spanish gypsy girl I knew. She read my tea leaves, or my navel—I've forgotten which—so I took a taxi to Southampton, got aboard the first American ship I saw and told them I wanted to go.

Later, when the Stukas bombed Coventry, I'm sure the attack was led by former German acrobats who had had dealings with that same theatre manager. I don't think they were after the Jaguar factory at all.

CHAPTER 10

Them!

I FIRST STARTED WRITING for comedians in 1939. Bob Hope had just begun a series for Pepsodent. I bumped into him one day in the street and he asked me if I'd like to write some jokes for his program. I was very flattered. He offered me fifty dollars a week. I hadn't worked for some time, and I had no money in the bank. I also had never written a joke in my life, but I held out for *sixty* a week. Bob, who in those days was not known as the philanthropist's philanthropist, finally came through, and I went to work for him.

Writing Hope's radio show was the greatest training a comedy writer could have, because Bob believed in competition writing; that is, pitting writers against each other to see who could come up with the best lines. And it was tough going, because, although we were all pretty green at it, Hope had an uncanny knack for picking writing talent, including myself. To hell with *modesty*—that's for strip teasers. Among the eight or ten writers employed by Hope at this time, there were Norman Panama and Melvin Frank, now one of Hollywood's big motion picture writing, producing and directing teams; Mel Shavelson and Jack Rose, who also became another of the famous motion picture W.P. & D. teams; a few others who have gone on to much fame and fortune; and a few who went nowhere, like the very talented Fred Williams, who, while bumming a ride, fell off a freight train near Truckee, California, and was killed. Incidentally, I told this story about Fred Williams on the air one night, and when I mentioned Truckee, I said it was *miles from nowhere*. This incensed the citizens of Truckee, so at this time I would like to apologize (belatedly) and put the record straight. Truckee, California, is not miles from *nowhere*. It's just fifty-eight miles from Grass Valley, California.

Bob Hope was very demanding and was never satisfied that he had enough comedy material from us, so in sheer desperation, the writers finally cooperated with each other (and it *takes* desperation to make writers do this) and decided that the single writers would write only twenty pages for each show, and the teams would write only forty pages. With eight writers—four singles and two teams—this would give Hope one hundred and sixty pages of material for a half-hour radio show, which could never run more than *twenty* pages.

This gave Hope a choice that would have been overwhelming to anyone else, but to him, the most unruffled comic in show business, it presented no problem at all. He just pencilled the lines he liked out of this mountain of material, and we would put it together somehow, and the show would go on. In later years, I was one of the writers on his television shows. By that time, the competition system was no longer in vogue. You wrote a sketch, handed it in and it was done the way it was written, except for the ending. Hope was never satisfied with the ending on *any* sketch that *anybody* ever wrote. He always thought it could be better. Sometimes he was right.

After Hope, in radio, there were Red Skelton, Jack Paar, Ozzie and Harriet (The Adventures of), Jimmy Durante and Garry Moore, Jack Carson, Dean Martin and Jerry Lewis, Johnny Carson and Phil Harris; and in TV, again there were Hope, Skelton, Paar and George Gobel. I won something called the "Emmy" for the Gobel show.

When I won the Emmy the committee made me sign a note promising that I would *never* sell it, but if I ever *did*, I must promise to sell it back to the committee, for forty dollars. One day, a year or so later, just for the hell of it, I called the Television Academy of Arts and Sciences, and told them I wanted to sell my Emmy. They said okay they'd give me thirty-five dollars for it. I asked what happened to forty? They said they were sorry but thirty-five was all they could pay for the Emmy. When I asked why, they said because it was "used."

One night during the war, I had just finished watching one of my radio shows at NBC in Hollywood, and now it was relax time at the Tropics, a fun place, just across from the studio on Vine Street. At that time *every* place jumped, but the Tropics really rocked, and in those days I rocked a little myself, especially after a show. Good, bad or indifferent, this was the time to get loaded. And in no time at all I was well on the way to hangoversville. The next morning, long before it was decent, I got a phone call from a Mr. Reber. Mr. John Reber of the J. Walter Thompson advertising agency. Mr. Reber wanted to know when I was going to bring the record down so he could hear it. What record, I wanted to know. He explained that last night I had mentioned an audition record I had made, with myself performing, which so far nobody had bought for a radio show. Well, I didn't remember mentioning this record to Mr. Reber last night, nor did I remember meeting Mr. Reber the night before, but I told him I would bring the record down just as soon as the fog lifted in the valley.

After Mr. Reber and his deadpan assistant, Joe Bigelow, listened to the record, they asked me if I'd like to be on a new show they were planning. The show was going to be called "What's New?" and they were going to use such people as Clark Gable, Jimmy Stewart, Gary Cooper, Walter Winchell, Louella Parsons, Hedy Lamarr, and just-name-anybody, plus me doing a comedy routine with Don Ameche as my straight man. Naturally, I said yes.

"What's New?" was a Saturday night show, and Saturday night was the loneliest night in the week—in radio. Even though we had every big star in the show business, plus many people from the outside world, such as J. Edgar Hoover and Bernard Baruch, the show didn't get much of a rating, and Mr. Reber decided to have the show originate from New York instead of Hollywood, where he could keep his eye on it. Immediately, Don Ameche quit. He didn't *want* to originate from New York. After that, and before we moved East, I had various straight men, including Chet Huntley, Dick Powell and (almost) Herbert Marshall. I say *almost* Herbert Marshall, because he balked at playing, as he put it, "*Abbott* to *my* Costello," which I thought was a very funny line. To replace Mr. Marshall the agency hired

Mr. Cecil B. DeMille. When my wooden-pussed friend, Joe Bigelow, gave me *this* news I almost flipped. I couldn't imagine getting laughs with this King-of-Kings-type straight man. Joe soothed me with a little absinthe his friend Toulouse had sent him, and I agreed to what I thought would be certain disaster. I couldn't have been more wrong. Mr. DeMille was the greatest straight man in the world. His dignity juxtaposed with my unruliness made everything seem twice as funny. His timing was perfect. He *knew* comedy. And he *worked* at it. By air time he was always letter perfect. Mr. DeMille was just as eccentric in his way as I was in mine. One night just before the show, he had arrived at the studio in a blue serge suit, but before he came onstage he changed into his corduroy coat, his riding breeches and his puttees; then he had the announcer say as he introduced him, "Mr. DeMille has asked me to apologize for his appearance, as he has just come in from his ranch."

The first "What's New?" show from New York was a shambles. But a shambles with a *master plan*. First, somebody hired somebody's cousin, who had always-wanted-to-be-a-radio-writer-but-nobody-would-ever-give-him-a-chance, to write the show. Then somebody hired the great Metropolitan Opera baritone, Leonard Warren, for the comedy bits. Then somebody else thought it would be a wonderful idea, "public relations-wise," to do the show in the auditorium of a local veterans' hospital.

The genius who picked this locale evidently hadn't asked too many questions, because the veterans who showed up on the night of the show weren't from any war that had happened lately. At any moment I expected Florence Nightingale to come tripping down the aisle and leaning over each one of them with her lamp, saying "Well, how do we feel to-night?" Flo didn't show but John Reber did—and announced that *he* was going to do the "warm-up." For those of you who don't already know, the warm-up is usually performed by a semi-funny announcer or the comedian on the show, and is supposed to warm the audience up to a frame of mind where they'll laugh and scream and pee in their pants in enjoyment of the show. As the head of the then, and it may still be, largest advertising agency in the world, Mr. Reber had a certain flair, but as an audience warmer-upper he was the bride at the funeral, the corpse at the wedding and the hair in the martini. It was like open house at the Birdseye plant—in a twinkling the whole group was quick-frozen. Solid. During the show I tried my best to thaw them out, but with Leonard Warren as my straight man, this was impossible. His magnificent baritone voice did not lend itself to comedy, and by the time he had finished thundering out the first funny question, the audience, who to a man wore hearing aids, had blown their tubes. As a consequence, they couldn't hear *my* funny answer. Not that it would have mattered much if they had, because I didn't have any G.I. jokes about Teddy Roosevelt or Stonewall Jackson or General Braddock, so I don't think they would have appreciated me anyway. After the show was over and the audience was being wheeled out, Mr. Reber tried his warm-up again just to see what was wrong with it. It didn't work this time either.

The next day after "Operation Omelet," as the newspapers called it, I decided I would be much better off back home, where the buffalo roam, and the deer and the antelope have ticks, than in the Big City, so I resigned, and that night while lounging in the booze car of the Twentieth Century Limited on my way back to California, I started reading *Billboard*, a theatrical trade paper. On the second or third page was reported the results of a poll which had been taken among some eight hundred radio editors around the country, and under the heading of "Outstanding New Start of 1943," I had been chosen as No. 1. Gee, I thought, that's pretty good, but it wasn't until after I had ordered Mogen David for everybody that I suddenly remembered— it was now 1944 and I was out of work.

🐴 🐴 🐴 JOHN REBER ISN'T WITH US ANY more, but wherever he is, I'm sure he's doing the warm-up.

But getting back to the *grim* business of writing *comedy*. There's nothing funny about sitting down at a typewriter with an acre of white paper in front of you, and trying to think of something that's gonna kill the people. Of course, it depends on who you're writing for, too—the degree of grimity, I mean. If you are knocking out funnies for some-one like Bob Hope, who has guts, it's not so bad. If you tell Bob that something is funny, he goes out and gives it everything he's got. But, unfortunately, most comedians have no confidence, either in the material, themselves or the audience. Consequently, if you tell comedian X or Y (Boy! am I playing it safe!) that something is funny, and he agrees to try it *against his will*, he usually "dogs" it; or, in plainer words, he doesn't do it well or with much confi-dence, so consequently it does not get a laugh. Then, he

59

comes off and immediately sneers: "Ya see—I toldja it was nothing!" *Confidence* is 75 per cent of the success of comedy delivery. If *you* believe, a lot of other people will, too. In the twenty-some odd (and how!) years I've been writing, I've heard the expression, "*Who* knows what's funny?" a couple of thousand times. And at the risk of getting belted in the mouth, I have answered every time: "*I* do." And I do. Writing comedy is an art, like plumbing. *Once* you *know* how to stop the toilet from overflowing, you can do it almost every time.

Jack Paar has a lot of confidence and a mind of his own; so does Ozzie Nelson, although I remember the time I brought in the first script I wrote for Ozzie. He read the whole thing without once changing the expression on his face. I felt like a juggler of Notre Dame auditioning for the Virgin Mary. As soon as I could escape, I called Al Scalpone of Young and Rubicam, and told him I wanted *out*, and right now. Al, who is a little on the nervous side anyway, almost had a litter right there and said he'd call me right back. When he did call he said Ozzie was *crazy* about the script and I should relax. Well, for a guy who was *crazy* about the script he sure had great control. I wouldn't want to be around if he wasn't *too keen* about a script. He probably stops breathing entirely. Nevertheless, after this first experience with the Silent Service, Ozzie and I got along fine, and, although I only stayed one year with the show (situation comedy is too pleasant a medium for me) we have been good friends ever since.

Red Skelton, one of the funniest clowns who ever lived (a phrase that everyone uses, but true), was easier to work for in radio than in television, I think probably because in the old radio days there was less pressure on him. I started writing for Red by simply telling him he needed me—which he did. He was doing a radio show from Chicago (a hot radio town then). I started by mailing him a few things. Then, when he came to Hollywood with an MGM contract, I went to work for him full time.

When Red first moved to California he bought a house in Tarzana, a town, named after guess-who, in the San Fernando Valley. Red was a wild do-it-yourselfer then and immediately started tearing the house apart and rebuilding it. I remember he bought some kind of papier-mâché wall covering that was supposed to look like red brick, but it didn't. It looked like papier-mâché wall covering that looked like the inside of the Count of Monte Cristo's cell in the *first* movie about this character. It was the most phony-looking material I'd ever seen, but Red went happily about his appointed task and covered the whole bottom half of the outside of his house with this stuff. I expected the neighbors to rise up in protest, but they didn't. Actually, in this particular neighborhood, *any*thing would have been an improvement. Red's judgment in real estate became better with the years, but his first venture in California was a mistake, and he didn't help it much with cardboard brick. And to top it all off, he built a five thousand-dollar swimming pool in his back yard. And this in a neighborhood where anybody with a three-dollar bird bath was considered a snot-nosed snob.

Red now lives in Bel Air, probably the most exclusive and expensive residential district in the world. Garbage must be gift-wrapped before it can be sent out. Even then there's no guarantee that it will be accepted. Bel Air is also famous for the Bel Air Grand Prix which is held every day. Colored maids driving station wagons. It's wild!

My first awareness of Dean Martin and Jerry Lewis came from Rufus Lemaire of Universal studios, whom I had gone to see about writing a movie. Mr. Lemaire told me about what kind of a movie he thought he wanted. Of one thing he was pretty sure: it was to be a comedy. And he rattled off a few names of the comedy people he thought should be in it. Joan Davis was one. There were quite a few others, most of them second-raters "moneywise"; then at the end of the list, he added, ". . . and two guys from New York that are supposed to be pretty funny."

Well, Martin and Lewis, the two guys from New York who were supposed to be pretty funny, finally arrived in Hollywood, but by that time they had been signed by Paramount and also by NBC, which was where I came into the picture—writing their radio show. I remember the first time I was supposed to meet them. I arrived at Robert L. Redd's office (he was the producer) when he suddenly started frothing at the mouth, because I had worn the wrong clothing! When he calmed down he explained to *me* that he had told *them* that I was a character who always wore a filthy trench coat with a big oil stain on the back, plus a twenty-foot red knitted scarf around my neck; and I had unwittingly turned up this day in a blue suit, minus my semi-filthy trench coat, and my *ten*-foot red knitted scarf. So far as Bob Redd was concerned, this was a major screw-up, but as I lived too far away to go get these props, he scurried around until he found someone else's filthy trench coat and a long knitted scarf, it was green, but this was an emergency. As it turned out, I sat around for about two hours in these character clothes, but neither Dean nor Jerry showed up. This opening bit sort of set the tenor of what was to come.

Like World War II, the Martin and Lewis radio show was under-rehearsed and therefore was less than a smash, but their movies, nightclub appearances and, later, their television shows were such enormous successes that Jerry's father, Danny Lewis, changed his name to Jerry Lewis, Senior.

This chapter could have been headed "Dolls and Bastards," but that might have been unfair because most of the comics I've dealt with have been dolls. There were only a couple of bastards. One bastard, who will have to be nameless (they are anyway, aren't they?), tried to hire me at a lot less than my established salary. This was during the war, so when I refused his unkind offer, he then tried his best to get my mother a gold star, but General Hershey informed him that although they were not yet ready to scrape the bottom of the barrel, he would keep me in mind, which I thought was sweet.

The other bastard will have to be nameless, too, because I can't remember who he was or what he did, but *he* knows what he *did* and *who* he is, so now it's become his problem— right, Sigmund?

But getting back to the dolls, Danny Thomas, for whom I once worked on a television variety series, fell in love with a monologue I had written for him, but two days later he hated it. Why? Because someone had gotten to him and told him it just wouldn't do. This someone, I found out later, was his agent, who was also *my* agent. I was astonished and deeply wounded. It was like being kicked in the family jewels by your own duenna.

63

But comedy material is always at the mercy of inexpert outside opinion, it seems. Jimmy Durante used to try out his show material on elevator operators, bellhops, taxi drivers or anybody else handy. If they didn't laugh, Durante would immediately lose confidence in it.

I was hired once to write for Bea Lillie, whom Noel and I adored and still do. Actually, I was hired to punch up, revise and modernize some of her old stage sketches for television. This I did, but when it came near air time, somebody —I don't know who—got chicken, and it was decided to leave the sketches in their 1928 pristine state. Maybe it was dear Lady Peel herself who decided not to change the tried and true, but I rather think it was some comedy expert like her hairdresser or her greengrocer or maybe her dibble-doubled damasked didder dapkins dealer. It doesn't matter. The sketches were performed. Everybody laughed. And the show was cancelled.

Another soul-searing, ambition-crushing experience happened to me on a show starring Ed Wynn, a very funny comic of the prop school of comedy. I had written a bit which required exactly seventy-eight television sets for use as prop stairs for Mr. Wynn to climb up to a second story window, say a line and climb down again. On the day of the show (props *never* arrived *before* the day of the show) I came into the studio, took one look at the stage and almost swooned dead away. They had, at the most, fifteen television sets as stairs, leading up to a second story window no more than four feet off the ground. As the whole point of this visual comedy bit depended on the vast number of television sets and the height Mr. Wynn had to climb to deliver his line, the revised arrangement meant absolutely nothing.

LEFT: *Mother with one of her pet werewolves*

(Lynbrook, 1924)

BELOW: *My first pair of short pants*

(Lynbrook, 1927)

ABOVE: *Buddy Rogers trying to get the band to drown me out (an impossibility)* (Chicago, 1933—CANDID PHOTO ILLUSTRATORS)

BELOW: *Bank stickup, anyone?*

(Red Skelton, Edna Skelton, and Little Me; Hollywood, 1940)

LEFT: *Come to me, my melancholy baby*

(Northridge, California, 1940)

BELOW: *Bing doesn't seem to be "relating" to me very well*

(Hollywood, 1943)

RIGHT: *Did you ever have one of those days?*

(Northridge, California, 1944)

BELOW: *Other writers work with people*

(Northridge, California, 1945 —GENE LESTER)

My great drive-in martini friend

(Lionel Barrymore at our housewarming party;
Northridge, California, 1948—GARBER STURGES)

ABOVE: *On tour—David Swift, Leo Solomon and I welcome ourselves to Jack Carson's home town*

(Carson, Dave, Leo and me, 1948)

BELOW: *Our new house in Northridge—the servant's swimming pool* (1948)

"I'll gladly cut anything you don't like out of the script, sir"

When I screamed to the director, he told me that *they* had thought fifteen television sets would be enough. When I tried to pin him down to who *they* were, he clammed up like a loser on "The Price Is Right!" I never found out who *they* were, and I could never understand why *they* didn't use seventy-eight television sets instead of fifteen, because, for one thing, the show was sponsored by RCA-Victor who were trying to sell television sets. Anyway, the bit didn't get a laugh. Seventy-eight television sets are a helluva lot funnier than fifteen—even an elevator operator or a bellhop or a taxi driver or a hairdresser or maybe even a producer knows that. But *they* didn't.

The "orange juice crisis" was something else that happened to me in my comedy-writing-for-television days. I had a line for Bob Hope on one of his shows in a sketch in which Bob was portraying a Southern plantation owner. At one point he pours himself a big shot of Bourbon, into a glass out of a Bourbon bottle, contemplates the glass for a moment, says to himself, "Hmmmm. Kentucky orange juice!" then drinks it down, presumably getting a good laugh from the studio audience. This all seems simple enough, doesn't it? How could it become a crisis or, more correctly, a tragedy? Well, easy. As I said before, stage props, liquids included, never seem to arrive in the studio until the last possible moment, and this show was no different from any other. The show was *live*, so anything that happened belonged to the ages. Hope started to do the Southern plantation owner in that sketch, everything going along fine and funny until he got to the bottle of Bourbon bit. He picked up the bottle, poured a big shot into a glass and said, on cue: "Hmmmm. Kentucky orange juice," but nothing happened. There was not even a suggestion of a snicker from the large studio audience, because the prop man, who suddenly that *very day* had started to *think*, had put *real orange juice* into the Bourbon bottle; and when Hope poured himself a glassful, the audience could see for themselves that it *was* orange juice and, for all they knew, it *could* have come from Kentucky, so what was so funny? Later, we writers got together and sent the prop man home in two shopping bags.

Another splendid example of the solidity of a statement I have made many times—i.e., that very few people are entitled to their opinions—was a matter of costuming. This also happened on a Bob Hope show. I had written a sketch featuring three hipsters in zoot suits. The right hipster and the left hipster were people, but the middle hipster was a *gorilla* also in a zoot suit. The crisis followed the pattern of the preceding ones, for I didn't get to see the hipsters in their costumes until the day of the show, when it's too late to change anything (naturally). The right hipster and the left hipster were costumed perfectly in their zoot suits, which I'm sure everyone agrees are pretty outlandish anyway, but the gorilla was wearing a "funny" zoot suit. It wasn't enough that a gorilla was wearing a zoot suit. The costume designer had added exaggerated shoulders (on a gorilla? ? ?), funny yellow shoes and a very small "funnied up" zoot hat with a very long and large plume sticking out of the hatband. The costume designer in one stroke had transformed what might have been the funniest bit of the year into the hokiest bit of *any* year. I found myself going from cast member to cast member and finally to the audience, one by one, explaining, with tears running down my cheeks (all four of them), that the gorilla's costume wasn't the way I had planned it. Please believe me. Please! Please! Please!

But enough of tragedy on the tube; let's get back to personalities.

My experiences with Jimmy Durante and Garry Moore, who were then a radio team, were quite pleasant, although we wound up in a law suit in which I sued them and lost. The way Jack Paar tells the story, Garry wanted me to write a sketch about Mothers, but I wrote a sketch about the Panama Canal instead. This is more or less true. Being a writer, I felt that I would know more about funny subject material, so I chose a more "comedic" line. As a consequence for going into business for myself, which I've never hesitated to do, Garry took umbrage and practically challenged me to a duel. One thing led to another in rapid succession, and I found myself fired.

The next scene took place in downtown Los Angeles, where nobody, except Doctor Finch and a few writers who are suing comics, ever goes. In court things didn't go well at all for me. The judge, who looked exactly like Edmund Gwenn (and it *could* have been), immediately fell in love with Jimmy Durante, and right then and there I knew I was sunk. The opposition lawyer, who was a real gallus snapper, almost gave himself breast cancer, but he won the case. And, it didn't take long for the judge to beat me over the head with a bladder, *figuratively* speaking, of course. It made me feel very badly, not only because I had lost, but it also was Christmas Eve and, I might add, a Christmas Eve I'll long remember, because it was the night that our house burned down.

CHAPTER 11

Christmas Eve
Cook-Out

CHRISTMAS EVE started out happily enough except for one thing: the house was on fire. But we didn't know it. Lionel Barrymore, a neighbor and godfather of my son, had stopped by on his way home from MGM, where he was at the time making a series of Doctor Kildare pictures, or as he called them: "Bedpan Operas." It was rather exhausting when Barrymore stopped by, because he could always only stay a minute and refused to get out of his station wagon, because of his physical condition (one of his legs wasn't so good). But although he could only stay a minute and wasn't supposed to drink, he never refused a martini. I always drank with him, but I had to stand at the side of the car while he was comfortably sitting at the wheel. That's why I said it was exhausting, but only for me. In those days I never counted the martinis, so I have no way of telling how many we had, but it was quite dark when Lionel decided to head for home, which was a ranch some five or six miles away at the end of a rather treacherous bit of road, which at one point ran through an extremely capricious stream. Sometimes it was a babbling brook, and at other times it was Niagara. When Lionel left, I said a little prayer that tonight it would be a babbling brook, because, no matter what, he would always drive through it as if he were escaping from Egypt with Pharoah tail-gating him. One rainy night he sat midstream in his station wagon with water up to his shoulders until some Boy Scout, who happened to be driving a tractor, came by and pulled him out. The Scout got a special merit badge for salvage.

After Lionel left, I went into the house and started a roaring fire in the fireplace. It was a corner fireplace and had always given us trouble in the smoke department. We had had every fireplace expert in the San Fernando Valley look at it, and they all agreed—it smoked. Some of the experts had actually worked on it, removing a few bricks here, or adding a few there. Nothing helped, and we resigned ourselves to evenings of partial asphixiation. Actually, I'm probably making a mountain out of a molehill, because it really wasn't too bad if you lay face down on the floor with your nose near a crack.

After a dinner of steak and some absorbent-type vegetables to sop up the martinis, we decorated the Christmas tree, said a "prayer for the boys over there" (we lived across the road from a horse breeding farm, and they had a whole barnful of jockeys) and went to bed.

The house was in the shape of an "L," enclosing a swimming pool. My bedroom was at one end of the "L," and I slept in a single bed with four dogs: two dachshunds named Anthony and Cleopatra, a Great Dane named Peter, and a hairy, insane mutt, named Gertrude. I never intended to bed down with Anthony, Cleopatra, Peter and Gertrude, but during the night, after I was well asleep, one by one they'd creep into bed with me. Anthony and Cleopatra curled around each other in between my legs (inside my pajamas), Gertrude snuggled her *wire*-haired head against my neck and Peter, the Dane flopped *across* my legs. In the morning, and I mean each and *every* morning, I would wake up at dawn, fresh as a dead daisy. But I hadn't the heart to tell them 1) that I didn't want them to sleep with me, 2) that they were dogs, and 3) that they were adopted. So that's the way it went until, of course, this particular Christmas Eve.

About two o'clock in the morning, the entire roof blew off the house in one tremendous, earth-jarring explosion, and the whole house was in flames. I jumped out of bed, opened the door to the outside, the dogs ran through it, then I raced through the hall to my son Johnny's bedroom. He was wide awake and jumping up and down in his crib. I grabbed him and made it out the door just as the roof collapsed. I had two cars in the garage, which was part of the house: a fifteen-year-old Pontiac coupé and a brand-new Buick convertible.

After making sure Johnny and my wife were safe, I dashed over to save the cars. The Buick wouldn't start. The fifteen-year-old Pontiac started immediately and I backed it out of the garage into the fields. By this time, somehow, the fire department had been notified, but when they arrived, they couldn't get in. I had two gates, a steel gate, out at the road, which was locked, and a huge wooden gate some five hundred feet beyond the first gate, also locked. The first gate presented no problem; they just lifted it off its hinges. But the second gate, which was eight inches thick, couldn't be budged. So they decided the only way they could get through would be by driving into it and tearing it off its hinges. The fire engine, a hook and ladder, by the way, backed off for a few hundred feet, then, revving up as high as it could, crashed through the gate. But, unfortunately, it was going a little too fast to stop, and suddenly we had a hook and ladder in our swimming pool.

Just about that moment bullets started whistling and whining around all of us. I had about ten thousand rounds of 30-calibre ammunition stored in the house, because of the imminent invasion, we Californians thought, by Japanese troops. This meant everybody back in the pool, which was the only safe place. It didn't take long for ten thousand rounds to go off in that heat, and the firemen got down to the business of trying to save a wall or two of what was left of the house, but suddenly there was a new menace; flying marinara sauce, pork and beans, corn beef hash, and other choice canned delicacies had become Molotov cocktails in the extreme heat. I had only that afternoon stocked up with about three hundred cases of black-market canned goods, all of which exploded and with much greater force than the 30-calibre ammo. If we'd only realized this, we probably could have shortened the war by a couple of years! However, with the dawning of Christmas Day, my wife started having another baby (prematurely) and was rushed to the hospital; I found one of the dachshunds, Cleopatra, suffocated under my bed, she'd evidently run back into the house in panic; the firemen went; and my eighteen-month-old son, the remaining three dogs, and I were left alone with a couple of acres of smouldering boards, beans and books, and a beautiful swimming pool, with a hook and ladder in it. Yes, Virginia, there *is* a Santa Claus.

CHAPTER **12**

Instant Gypsies

I HAVE HEARD that Toulouse-Lautrec was very superstitious. For one thing, he would *never* walk under a black cat. I'm the same way now. I mean—superstitious. Never again will I trust a corner fireplace. That had been our undoing. The fireplace. The man from the Arson Squad explained the whole thing to me. Our corner fireplace had been tampered with by the experts so much that gradually the bricks that kept the heat away from the wooden walls had been removed, so that every time we lit a fire the wood kept charring—never quite catching fire—charring just enough so that finally something akin to spontaneous combustion occurred. The fire travelled up through the walls and into the attic, where it spread rapidly and also built up a terrific gas pressure which finally exploded.

So much as to "why." Now as to "who." My first visitor that Christmas morning was Lionel Barrymore, who said, "What's new?" Later on, he came back and brought me a beautiful suit of clothes that he'd had made in London, about thirty-five years before, I guessed. As I had nothing except a singed bathrobe to wear, I put this outfit on, and I looked exactly like I was wearing a suit that Lionel Barrymore had bought thirty-five years ago in London. My second visitors were neighbors Desi (Arnaz) and Lucille (Ball), who said, "What's new?" Later, they came back and brought hot soup, which seems to be the standard palliative for victims of *any* tragedy. I'm just thankful that Desi didn't bring me a suit that he had had made thirty-five years ago in Cuba. Skelton came by next and said, "What's new?" Later, he also came back with hot soup and a sign reading: "Smokey the Bear Is Mad at You."

Later on in the day, the hot soup bit began to pall, and I decided that Johnny and I would have to have a place to sleep that night. Most people would have thought of a hotel or a motel, but not me. *I* bought a *trailer*. For thirty-five hundred dollars cash. Provided it was delivered that afternoon. It was, but there had been a few substitutions or maybe I should say *changes* and substitutions. In place of the brand-new white sidewall tires, there were four of the mangiest looking pieces of round rubber I had ever seen. They had been taken directly off a Mexican school bus. The little wheel on the front of the trailer was missing entirely. The shiny chrome finish that I had bought had now become chipped silver paint. The interior had changed quite a bit, too—the toilet was now in the living room. When I put up a fight, the two gorillas delivering this swindle told me to check out the numbers on my sales slip against the numbers on the trailer. They checked out all right. So, as Mother used to say, "They had me by the ass."

The Christmas tree I had bought at the same place (they sold *them* too), and for which I had paid seven dollars, on Christmas Day yet, was the same one I had picked out, strangely enough, and on it they had pinned an envelope. When I opened the envelope there was a note—no, not a thank-you note, just a note saying they had included a dozen business cards (Trailer City) and would I pass them out to anyone I knew who might be interested in a trailer or a Christmas tree or both. I have just remembered the name of the woman I dealt with at Trailer City. It was Ilse Koch. I wonder what ever happened to her?

Living in a trailer, no matter what the ads say, is for retired people. I guess maybe that's what the ads *do* say. You *have* to be retired—retired to the point where you're not able to move much. Because if you move much in a trailer you bump into people, and this causes friction. Not fun friction. Irritation friction. Which can lead to fist fights. And a fist fight in a trailer can be extremely frustrating, because you tend to hit everything but your opponent, and also your footwork is limited with a toilet in the middle of the living room. But there was nothing we could do about it; we were stuck with the trailer until we could build a new house. One day, while I was still alone, I hired a reformed lush nurse to take care of Johnny, and the first time I left her alone with him I came home a couple of hours later to find her passed out cold on the trailer steps, and Johnny in the pool, going down for the third time. I got him out, had a couple of my friends package the nurse for a trip to the drunk tank, and went out to get the mail. Besides the Sears Roebuck catalogue, I got my draft notice. I immediately

75

started to sing, "What a day this has been, What a swell mood I'm in, Why, it's almost like falling in love . . ." Then I placed a bow and arrow in my mouth, and pulled the trigger.

CHAPTER 13

Uncle Sam Needs Me?

AFTER SEEING WORLD WAR II in the newsreels I wasn't too anxious to go, but my draft card said 1-A, so I pulled a few strings there, used a little influence here, and the first thing I knew I was bending over naked at the reception center. Unfortunately, I had something wrong with me, I never knew what, and I was turned down, or was it turned *up?*— and told to go home.

When I got back to our little trailer home in the West, the head of the local draft board (who was a doll by the name of Bela Lugosi) called and suggested that now I had been refused by the armed forces maybe I should do something else for the war effort. When I volunteered to shoot Japanese snipers from out of the tops of the palm trees along Rodeo Drive in Beverly Hills, he said no, that wasn't what he had in mind. What he had in mind was that I use some of my vast estate (almost twenty-three acres) to raise something. When I said "How about chinchillas?" he said, "No. How about hogs?" When I protested that women weren't wearing much hog fur that season, he stopped me with "You wanna find yourself on Guadalcanal, Sweetie?" I had never heard of Guadalcanal, but it didn't sound too kosher, so I said, "Okay, hogs it is."

First, before I bought one single brood sow, not that they *have* to be single, I had to build a hog barn, a feed storage barn and several concrete pens complete with wading pools for the hogs. Just like the Fontainebleau, eh Mannie? After this extremely expensive construction was completed, I bought the stock: forty-eight Duroc brood sows and three boars. Durocs are a reddish brown color and withstand the hot California sun better than the lighter-colored hogs. (Stay outa the sun, Mannie.)

Only three boars with forty-eight sows may seem like an unfair ratio, to the sows, but let me be the first to assure you it ain't. It seemed like no time at all, and it wasn't, that the sows were having pigs all over the place, and in passing let me mention a strange thing. Sows always seem to farrow (have pigs) when it rains and at night. And, of course, when it rains, the hog barn leaks and gets the little pigs cold, and little pigs aren't supposed to get cold, so you take them into your own home to warm them up. I remember one night, and it *was* a night to remember, we had over fifty pigs warming up in the trailer. We had them in the oven, under blankets in bed, wrapped in quilts and huddled around demijohns filled with hot water, and also under infrared lamps. We really had wall-to-wall pigs. But it was worth it, I thought. If you can keep a little pig alive for the first few hours, it stands a good chance of staying alive up until the time its mother either lies down on it or steps on it. Sows with pigs are kept in tiny seven-by-seven-foot enclosures with guard rails on all four sides to prevent the sow from flopping down on her own flesh and blood, but accidents happen, and very, *very* frequently, and to be quite frank about mother love in Swineland, it doesn't mean a thing. I have seen many a four-hundred-pound "mother" flop down on one or two of her little ones, and they can squeal their squeals off and she won't move her lard *one inch*. As a result, of all this reverse matricide, out of a litter of ten to fourteen pigs, if seven or eight reach maturity it's miraculous.

I don't know whether my raising hogs shortened the war any, but it *did* shorten my bank account. During the war the price of hogs was frozen at fifteen dollars per hundred pounds, but the price of corn was unfettered. As a consequence, the cost of *feeding* the hogs outdistanced the market price by about two to one. After I had lost approximately twenty thousand dollars (not counting barns, etc.) I went out of the hog business—abruptly. Some misguided soul from San Diego came up and bought my entire stock, by this time over a thousand hogs of various sizes. And to tell you the truth, I felt like a father, watching truckload after truckload leave for the south. *My* children going to live with *strangers*. The next morning, however, when I looked at the market report on the price of corn, I felt less like a father and more like a cat with a bellyful of canaries.

CHAPTER 14

Hollywood Joins The Allies, *and Other War Stories*

DURING THE WAR, they had something for the boys called the Armed Forces Radio Service. The West Coast headquarters for the Armed Forces Radio Service was located at a Fox motion picture studio at the corner of Sunset Boulevard and Western Avenue, in Hollywood. The Post (I think they called it a post) was headed by Colonel Tom Lewis, whose previous command had been at Fort Young & Rubicam. There were several other officers at the Sunset and Western post, most of whom had come from other advertising agencies. All of the enlisted men, none of whom had enlisted, were famous Hollywood motion picture and radio writers. A few had been through basic training, but apparently very few, because one day they were all told to report at the firing range for rifle practice. This, as it turned out, was the first, last and only rifle practice ever attempted by this group. From all reports it had been a second Pearl Harbor, but with *us* against *us*. These kids were never ever given anything that even resembled a weapon from that day on. Even sharp shoelaces became taboo.

I had belonged (as a civilian) to the Armed Forces Radio Service since it began, and I wrote radio programs that were to be beamed to the men overseas. It was an easy thing to do, and it didn't interfere with my regular radio writing jobs—just as being in the Army, at Sunset and Western, didn't interfere with anybody there working on *civilian* radio shows. It wasn't unusual at a civilian radio show writers' meeting to have three quarters of the staff in army uniforms. It was a handy arrangement, and rarely, so far as I knew, were any of these Hollywood writers sent overseas, except when they goofed off at their regular Army writing assignments. Then, someone would walk by them singing softly "Goodbye, Mamma, I'm Off to Yokahoma," which was a song during the war and gave you a gentle hint of how the fortune cookie was crumbling.

One of the jobs I had at AFRS was the writing, for the Office of War Information, of propaganda jokes or stories that were to be dropped by planes into occupied or enemy territory. This was supposed to be a very good way of demoralizing the enemy. I can remember only one joke that was supposed to be dropped into Germany. It went:

> FIRST GERMAN: "Isn't it nice that Denmark is co-operating with Germany so well? They are sending us butter and also steel."

SECOND GERMAN: "Yah—and both in the same
package."

I must explain that this joke, or sardonicism, was based on
the fact that Denmark *had* been supplying Germany with
butter, under pressure of course, but in many cases tiny
pieces of steel were found in it, thus making *all* Danish
butter suspect. I don't know how much the Germans were
demoralized by this type of stuff. Personally, with me, butter is taboo. Steel, my doctor says—*all* I can eat.

Most of the time in Hollywood, while I was writing for
either radio or television, I also worked as a script doctor for
the movies. That is, I would take someone else's script and
punch it up with funny lines. A script doctor never got any
credit on the screen. There's some kind of Screen Writers'
Guild ruling that says you must write at least (I think)
33⅓ per cent of the script to see your name on the screen.
You *can* take an "Additional Dialogue by" credit if you
want it, but as I understood this, it didn't do your writing
career any good to be known as an additional dialogue
writer. Anyway, I worked on all of Bob and Bing's early
"Road" pictures at Paramount, all of Skelton's earlier pictures at MGM, and at one time or another for most of the
other studios. Sometimes I worked at the studios, but most
of the time I took the scripts home with me and worked on
them in my spare time.

I didn't particularly relish the job of working on someone else's script, because you had to stick too close to what
they had already done. You couldn't dream up some new
scene, which required another set, because when you got
the script it was usually too late to build another set. Or too

82

costly. Or maybe you'd rewrite some scene that the producer had been crazy about the way it was.

Most of the writers at the film studios have had odd experiences, and so did I. At MGM I had an office of my own choosing. I didn't want to be in the Thalberg building where most of the writers, and producers were, because someone had warned me I'd be haunted by the brass if I were too close to them, so I picked an office in the old writers' building. And it *was* old. My office was situated on the main artery between the men's room and another writer's office, and this boy had very weak kidneys. I don't know how he ever got anything done, unless he had a typewriter in the can, too. Nevertheless, I got a little tired of him picketing me while I was working, so I requested a new door and passage arranged—for him, so he wouldn't have to go through my office every time he got the call. The new door and passage took about two weeks to complete. They had to blast through several walls. On the happy day this mammoth project was finished, and I was alone at last, I got my notice. They no longer needed my services at MGM.

At RKO, I worked for Eddie Cantor, who was producing a picture there. Mr. Cantor, according to reports from the writers who worked for him, was given to tantrums if things weren't going well. Maybe this was true, I don't know. At RKO he was very calm and considerate, and although most of the story conferences I had with him consisted mainly of monologues about show business, and very little about the picture he was making, I found him a most interesting man. I made one mistake with Mr. Cantor: I didn't particularly care for a girl he had chosen for one of the smaller parts in the picture, and told him she inspired me not. How the hell did *I* know it was one of his daughters?

Jack Cummings, a producer at MGM, is a man I'll always remember with warmth. I doubt very much if he remembers *me* working for him, but there came a day, in his office, when he rescued me from a murder rap. A director, who shall be anonymous and who is even more so today, was reading my script changes to Mr. Cummings, and at every script change that I had made this director suggested something else in its place, and his suggestions came right out of a book called *Encyclopedia of Comedy,* which was written in 1895 "For professional entertainers, social clubs, comedians, lodges and all who are in search of humorous literature." This untalented churl had *memorized* the book. I was about to chop him in the head and drop him out the window, when Mr. Cummings stopped him with, "I think we'd better leave Jack's changes the way they are and get on with the picture, because we're running out of time." As I said before, I'm sure Mr. Cummings doesn't remember this incident, but the director didn't speak to me from that moment on, and hasn't to this day. How lucky can a guy get?

I don't know how the Hollywood studios operate today, so far as the writers are concerned, because I haven't lived there for about four years, but when I was working on motion picture scripts, most of the other writers frowned on eager beavers. I remember once, early in my script-doctoring career, some writer, who was apparently the spokesman for the rest of them, came into my office and said: "What the hell are *you* trying to prove?" When I asked him what the *hell* he meant, he said: "Ya handed in ten pages yesterday!" When I said, "What's wrong with that?" he said, "Two or three pages is plenty. You hand in ten

84

pages a day and you'll be outa work in a week! You're gonna kill the whole racket!" Well, I saw his point, and slowed down a little, although it was contrary to my nature to write slowly. Actually, I wrote just as much, but I didn't hand it all in at once. This system, although it sounds dishonest, really isn't. If it were possible to write a full script, and a *great* script, in three days, and you handed it in to the producer on the fourth day, no matter how great the script was, he would have no respect for it, because it didn't take a long time to write. For instance, on Broadway, some of the greatest hits have been written in a week, and no play should ever take over a month to write. They *do* take longer than this to write. Much longer. Because most writers are stallers. They'll do anything to avoid sitting down to write. Research. That's *always* a good excuse not to write.

Nordhoff and Hall, when they wrote *Mutiny on the Bounty*, did a tremendous research job, even to having a complete and exact model of the *Bounty* sent to them from England. So what was the story? A mutiny on a ship. The Captain and a few men set adrift in a lifeboat, and the mutineers winding up at Pitcairn Island. *This* you can find out in any encyclopedia with five minutes reading. They didn't have to find out what kind of a man Captain Bligh was. He was exactly like *every* ship captain of that era. A despot. What about the ship? Why was it necessary to know exactly what the ship looked like? For the technical names of each part of the ship? Who would know what you were talking about? Do you know what a Straus heel-type trunnion is? It's a certain type of bridge (there's one over the Chicago River). That's the *technical* name for it. The bridge on the River Kwai, or the bridge that they blew up in *For Whom the Bell Tolls,* do you know what kinds of bridges they were? Do you care? Neither does the writer, but it's fun to look at pictures and read descriptions of bridges all over the world. Do you know what these words refer to: simple? abruptly pinnate? odd pinnate? twice odd pinnate? pinnately decompound? palmate? dentate? crenate? entire? serrate? doubly serrate? pinnately lobed? palmately lobed? undulate? They sound, to *me,* like fun positions during intercourse, but actually they're *leaf* forms. I wonder if the composer of "The Falling Leaves" researched leaf forms before he sat down at the piano. If he didn't, he should have. We could have had a nice dirty song about falling leaves. It would have *made* Belle Barth! But enough of this ranting about the value of research. In the first place, it's very presumptuous of me, having never written a Broadway play or a serious book; and in the second place, I'm getting off the subject of writing for the movies.

Writing for the movies, now, is a very specialized business. If you're writing an $18,000,000 pseudo-biblical extravaganza, you've got to figure out a way to get in more naked girls and *more crucifixions.* The movies have come a long way since *Spartacus,* with its measly six hundred. You also have to figure out more grisly ways to do away with the hero. For instance, just the other day some writer had a brilliant idea. "Why not," he asked, "have Steve McQueen beat Kirk Douglas to death with Charlton Heston?" Why not?

Financing of motion pictures has grown a lot more complicated in recent years, too, mainly because of the enormous salaries the stars are receiving. They're making a picture right now, starring Elizabeth Taylor and Frank Sinatra, for which *each* of them is getting 100 per cent of the gross (and 50 per cent of anything over that!).

That's why many motion pictures are now being made in Italy. To save money. Every drugstore in Rome sells movie film, and they develop it free!

But seriously though, as the leader of the partisans said as he was hanging Mussolini up by his heels, motion picture writing has improved considerably lately, primarily, I think, because the quality of the stars has risen considerably, too. It seems to me it would be very hard to write *badly* for Tommy Sands or Fabian or Paul Anka or Sandra Dee or Tuesday Weld or Chubby Checker or Conway Twitty.

I've never attempted to write an entire motion picture, but I have lots of ideas filed away in my "Things-to-do-in-the-future" book. I have one idea in particular that I know would sell, if I just took a few days off to write it up. There's this submarine, see. It's one of those atomic jobs that submerges for two years at a stretch, and at the end of the first year they discover that one of the crew is a girl in disguise, and she's five months pregnant. Then they have to find out who the father is, and there's a big scene like in *The Caine Mutiny.* Remember where the Captain is trying to find out who swiped the strawberries? Well, of course in my story he's trying to find out something else, but it's the same idea and if it worked once, it'll work again. The wind-up of the picture could be where the baby is born and it looks just like the Captain—mustache and all.

Then I have another idea. . . .

CHAPTER 15

Taj Mahal West

WHEN WORLD WAR II was presumably over, I planted ivy in my air raid warden's helmet and started to think about my life. After about twenty minutes I decided to emigrate to Tahiti. I wrote to the American consul (they don't have one any more) in Papeete. His reply, which took about two months to reach me, was very discouraging. It seems that after the war, rich French refugees had swarmed over the place, pushing the prices up and generally spoiling the whole idea of easy living in the South Seas. There were no regular ship schedules to Tahiti. And, of course, no air lines then; and if you wanted any dental work done you had to go to Honolulu or San Francisco. Just my luck, I didn't have a dentist in Honolulu, so the whole picture looked pretty dark, so far as living out the rest of my life as a part-time beachcomber. (The rest of the time I was going to write radio shows and send them by wireless back to the States.) When this dream blew up, I decided to give California another chance and build a new house, this time a fireproof one.

I consulted with a few architects, and, of course, the one whose ideas I liked best was Welton Beckett, who has since gone on to be world-famous in his profession. I have always felt as if I discovered Mr. Beckett, because although he was known only locally then, I recognized his great talent and never missed an opportunity to mention it. Welton Beckett didn't design my new house. *I* did.

In the first place, in order to have a house that was fireproof, it had to be built entirely out of concrete blocks with the exception of the roof, which it was. And for double insurance, because of the wooden roof, the house was built in separate sections, like a powder magazine. If one section blew up or, in our case, caught fire, it wouldn't take the whole place with it. This meant, of course, that the bedrooms were separated from each other and also separated from the main house, but connected by eight-foot cement block walls.

The main house contained a thirty-by-fifty-foot living room with a fireplace you could stand up in and which could hold ten-foot logs. At a forty-five degree angle off the living room was the billiard room, and angled off the other end of the living room was a twenty-foot bar with the kitchen behind it. Between the main house and the bedrooms was a Noguchi-table-shaped swimming pool with three-thousand-watt underwater floodlights and a special sunken plate glass window for underwater photography. The pool was also equipped with many sprays with colored lights playing on them, and on the bottom of the pool a gorgeous nude wriggled enticingly. This was done by projecting a

89

color slide from a hidden projector; the movement of the water gave her the wriggle.

The other two sections of the house contained two bedrooms and one bathroom each. The bedrooms had clear glass roofs covered by a shade during the day, but pulled back at night so you could lie back in bed and look at the stars. The bathrooms were fabulous, with infrared, ultraviolet and other kinds of lights, making a total of nine in each bathroom. The bathtubs were large and sunken and had an array of showers and sprays that hit every part of your body. We even had plain *water*, if that's what you wished.

Next to my bed there was an electrical control panel which controlled every light in the house and the floodlights outside. With one flip of my bedside main switch, I could blow every circuit breaker at Boulder Dam.

Outside, on our twenty-three acres, I had planted trees from all over the world, but mostly evergreens, because there weren't many in Southern California. These trees, some of which were only a foot high and cost twenty-five or thirty cents, eventually grew to be fifty and sixty feet high and equally wide. At that time I had the largest redwood grove outside of Sequoia National Park.

The house took a year to build and cost over a hundred thousand dollars, and in its sylvan setting was truly a beautiful and unusual place. The day it was finished, I had to leave on a road trip to wet-nurse a comedian. Sometimes things happen when you're away on the road. And something *did* happen. Something blonde. I never went back.

CHAPTER 16

Should I Make Barbara Pregnant?

ONE DAY, a year or so after leaving California, I found my-self living with a *new group* in Locust Valley, Long Island, New York. Locust Valley, Long Island, New York is a charming place, especially if you don't mind people shout-ing "Tally-ho" under your window early Sunday mornings, as they chase some poor nonresident fox across your front lawn.

After about six months or so of this persecution of a mi-nority, we decided to move to Bucks County, Pennsyl-vania, which, of course, needs no further introduction. Everybody must have read at least *one* dirty book about Bucks County. We moved to the then, and still, unfashion-able part of Bucks County, Upper Black Eddy, on the west-ern bank of the Delaware River, just across from Milford, New Jersey, which was the closest metropolis.

For twelve thousand dollars, we bought a hundred and fifty acres of land, a small house, a huge barn and many outbuildings. The house and the barn had been built some two hundred years before, out of stone, with slate roofs. As I said, the barn was huge—large enough for a three-ring circus plus a midget auto race, and still room for a few polo ponies. The house was something else again. It was very small, and had originally been built, I had the forged and antiqued bills of sale to prove it, by Dutch settlers, who were *small* people. As a consequence, every time you went through a doorway you fractured your skull. Just a little, of course, but it added up.

There was no bathroom, so we went to work on that, first hiring a couple of plumbers, who were also electricians, carpenters, mechanics, midwives or anything that was needed. As plumbers, they were very strange: money meant *nothing* to them. Maybe they were just psychos. Anyway, they worked for two dollars an hour, and I had the good sense not to ask questions.

As there is no general sewerage system in Bucks County, we had to have a septic tank. A septic tank is a large hole in the ground, lined with concrete, and with numerous tunnels going off in several directions, for drainage. To dig this hole we hired a local eighty-year-old man. He looked about fifty, and he worked as if he were thirty. We were away for most of the first day when he was digging the hole, which had to be eight feet by eight feet by eight feet deep. When we got home, it was dark, and he was still digging. When he saw us, he straightened up with some difficulty and apologized for not having the job done, but he had encountered a few stones, which took time to remove. I still don't know how he did it—some of the stones must have weighed a hundred and fifty or sixty pounds apiece and had to be lifted from the bottom of an eight-foot hole. Another pyscho? I don't know, but he had the whole job, fifty-foot tunnels and all, done in three days.

Budd Schulberg lived in Upper Black Eddy, but we never met him. But we *did* meet Mrs. *Ulm*. Or I should say *I* met Mrs. Ulm—the first time. I was sitting at my typewriter, wax plugs in my ears to drown out any distraction, when I looked up and suddenly discovered myself in the same room with an apparition. It was Mrs. Ulm. She weighed about 250 pounds and was wearing a mangy fur jacket. I assumed she'd flown in through the window, but she told me she'd knocked on the door and I hadn't heard her. She said, "I would like to have your children." Well, this sounded as if we could do business, so I asked her to have a drink, but she said she couldn't stay because she had to take her husband's lunch to him, and that he was in the death house at the State Prison a few miles away in Easton. I thought about this for a moment. I thought it wasn't tough enough to be in the death house—they didn't even furnish lunch. As it turned out, her husband was a guard in the death house, and she went on to explain that *she* was a cousin of Veloz and Yolanda or the DeMarcos or somebody like that, and she taught dancing—classical dancing, that is—and also the piano, the violin, the saxophone, the clarinet, the trombone, the trumpet, the harp and, I presumed, a little practical withcraft. The purpose of her visit (outside of casing the place) was to find out if we would like the children to learn one or all of these essential arts.

When I asked her if she could teach someone to dance

93

"Swan Lake" and play the trombone at the same time, she said that's *just* what she had in mind. I could see right there and then that Mrs. Ulm was not to be, as they say in Upper Black Eddy, screwed around with. I told her that I would "speak to the Mrs." and she bowed low—as if she were either being presented at court or the ballast in her breasts had suddenly shifted—thanked me, and warped gently through the door.

I met *Mr.* Ulm under quite different circumstances. It happened one night when everybody had gone to the movies over in Milford. Everybody except me. I was sitting home staring at the wall, trying to figure whether I should make Barbara pregnant or not. This was a tough problem because Barbara wasn't my wife. She was Herbert's wife. Herbert was a wealthy shoe manufacturer, and Barbara and Herbert were two characters in a drama I was writing. The reason the problem was tough was that Barbara already had six children, which I thought was enough. But I had to get her out of the picture for a little while so Herbert could fool around with Gladys, a hot little dish, who was working as Herbert's secretary but who *really* was a spy for *Harry Karl* and had been *planted* with *Herbert's* firm to *steal* the *plans* for a new sharp toe that Herbert had in mind. After an hour of staring, coffee drinking and ad lib scratching, I decided that I *would* make Barbara pregnant. Then I had the problem (for the seventh time) of how should she let him know? Knitting tiny garments? I'd done that twice. Throwing up at breakfast? lunch? dinner? No. Strange food cravings—for shark fins or tapioca pudding? I didn't think so. Finally, I decided that she should stay in character—be shy about it. I had her run up to Her-

94

bert, while he was shaving (with a straight razor), and scream in his ear, "Herbert, you old bastard, you've done it again!" Now she was not only pregnant, but a widow as well. An excellent complication.

I turned on the eleven o'clock news and rewarded myself with a beer. I hoped the news would be gory and it was. One air liner crash. One fourteen-year-old boy had killed his adoring mother. And there had been a prison break at Easton. One George Mueller, a lousy name for a gangster, had escaped. He was a convicted murderer. He had a tattooed groin. He was armed, considered dangerous, and should be approached with caution—especially, I thought, if you wanted to see his tattooed groin.

After the news, I got back to pregnant Barbara. I didn't know whether to give her a girl or a boy this time. I chose a boy—for a reason: I thought maybe when *he* got to be fourteen he could knock off Barbara. While I was giving this *very little* thought, I became more and more aware of a short, intermittent howling. Another fox has blown his cork, was my first impression. There had been quite an epidemic of rabid foxes in Pennsylvania that year. But as the howling got closer, I realized the sounds came from bloodhounds. I had seen *I Am a Fugitive from a Chain Gang* only the night before on the early movie, so I knew what bloodhounds sounded like. I thought to myself, "Jesus, it's taken Paul Muni a helluva long while to get from Georgia to Bucks County." Then suddenly I thought about the escaped con. Maybe they were looking for *him!* But why in Upper Black Eddy? It really wasn't much of a place for harboring escaped murderers, unless of course, I thought, maybe Budd Schulberg had a hobby. After a while, the howling died out, and I got back to my typewriter. No sooner had I and Barbara given birth to her seventh child, when the door opened and a man leading two very muddy bloodhounds walked in. He had a large automatic pistol in his belt and a twelve-gauge shotgun tucked under his arm. We stared at each other for a moment or so; then he suddenly pointed the shotgun at me and said, "Just sit there—and don't try anything funny." I said, "Wait a minute. I'm not the guy they're looking for," and he said, "No—but *I* am." I said "Oh!" Then I just sat there, desperately trying not to do anything funny and also trying to think of mutual friends, when *suddenly* I *remembered*. "Do you know Mr. Ulm?" I said, beaming.

"Who?"

"Mr. Ulm," I said, "He's a—a Screw—up at the Big House."

"A *What—where?*"

I gave up this Warner Brothers talk and said, pointing at the dogs, "How come?"

"They're bloodhounds," he said.

"I know," I said. "But how come they're with you instead of with the cops?"

"People have got the wrong idea about bloodhounds," he said. "They just *sniff* until they findja—then they're supposed to yip until the cops get there—but these two," he went on, fondly stroking their wrinkled brows, "are just dopes."

"Where are the cops now?" (I thought—it's better to *know!*)

"Oh, they're around pretty close."

Trying to make it as offhand as possible, I said, "What are your—future plans?"

Just then a car pulled up in front of the house and stopped. We looked at each other. Then he pointed the shotgun right at my belly. A pretty unimaginative target. There was a knock at the door. At a gesture from my uninvited guest, I asked, "Who's there?"

"It's Mr. Ulm," a voice answered.

"It's Mr. Ulm," I whispered to the shotgun wielder.

"Who?"

"Mr. Ulm. He's a Screw up at the Big——."

"Oh shit!" he said. "Don't start *that* again! Tell him to go away."

"Mr. Ulm," I said. "Er—I'm busy now. Can you come back later or tomorrow or—sometime?"

Another car pulled up and stopped. The escaped killer really looked worried now. "Who's that?" he said. I peeked through the blind. "It's my wife and kids."

"Holy Jesus," he said. "What *is this—a convention?*"

I said, "They *live* here."

He said, "Oh—yeah."

There came another knock at the door. "Come on, Jack —open up!" It was my wife.

"Has Mr. Ulm gone?" I said.

"No."

"He's with you?"

"Yes."

"Look," I almost yelled. "Why don't you and Mr. Ulm go have a drink!"

"What about the kids?" she said, suddenly becoming very logical.

"Drop them off at school. Let 'em be early for once."

"Look, Curley," she said. "What the hell's going on in there?"

"I'm being interviewed by *Time* magazine. Go away!" I screamed.

There was a long silence after this. Or, as they say in the collection department of the phone company, a long, *ominous* silence. I looked at the killer, and he looked at me. "Okay," he said, finally. "Open the door."

"You're not gonna shoot 'em down in cold blood!"

"Look, Mister," he said, patiently. "In the first place, there's no such thing as *cold* blood, and in the *second* place. . . . Oh nuts! Open the door."

I opened the door, and my wife, the two kids and Mr. Ulm came in. None of them were the least bit disturbed.

"Hi, Clarence!" said the killer, handing the shotgun and the automatic to Mr. Ulm.

"Thanks, Charlie," Mr. Ulm said.

"Charlie???"

"Yeah," said Mr. Ulm. "This here's Charlie Pearl. He's a trusty up at Easton. Every once in a while we send him out for cigarettes, and he forgets to come back. He lives here in Upper Black Eddy—when he's home."

"But what about this escaped murderer?" I asked. "It was all over the radio. This George Mueller. What about him?"

"Oh, they got him in about a half an hour," Mr. Ulm said. "I was on my way home, so I told 'em I'd pick up Charlie here. Incidentally, Charlie, where'd you get the shotgun and the pistol?"

"Bought 'em," said Charlie.

"At this time of night?"

"From Mr. Schulberg."

"Oh," said Mr. Ulm.

"Can I watch television?" said one of the kids.

"No!" said his mother, his brother, his father, Mr. Ulm and Charlie.

CHAPTER 17

Back To Monkey Island

WE HAD BEEN LIVING in the Bucks County farmhouse for about two months. The kids were enrolled in a little one-room country schoolhouse, where they had to kiss the teacher each morning, as they reported in (an old Quaker custom); our dogs were happy chasing rabbits; the house was beginning to shape up. We had ripped out a wall and found another enormous fireplace, and the new indoor toilet was just about ready for a test shot when I got a wire from Red Skelton in Hollywood. Red was entering the television scene and wanted me to write for him. But, of course, I couldn't do it by remote control. I would have to go to California.

That evening, as the sun was going down, I sat on the back porch of our cosy little farmhouse, and looked out at the lovely Pennsylvania countryside. The trees had just started to turn a little, and the air was tinged with a sort of purple haze. It was so quiet and so peaceful. I thought about Hollywood—and California. Did I want to go back? I really didn't know. Of course there were a few things about Hollywood I had missed. For instance, those wonderful weekends at Palm Springs where I used to go to cure my suntan. And I'd missed Darryl Zanuck. Although I'd never met him, it was a comfort to know that he was *there*. And I'd missed the guy who used to drive a convertible Cadillac Eldorado—a wild-looking blonde next to him, an enormous Great Dane in the back seat, and towing a forty-foot Chris-Craft Cruiser up and down Sunset Boulevard every Sunday afternoon. I never knew him *either*, but I *admired* him— anybody who loved dogs like he did.

And there were other things I had missed without realizing it. I had missed seeing all those fat-butted car hops at the drive-ins, who imagined they were starlets between pictures; and all those *thin*-butted car hops who imagined they were starlets between pictures; and all the medium-butted starlets between pictures, who imagined they were medium-butted starlets between pictures, but who were actually call girls between calls. I also missed seeing Monkey Island, which was sort of a forerunner of Disneyland. Monkey Island was the grandiose scheme of somebody's, which didn't quite come off; although they had thousands of monkeys running all over a man-made island in the middle of a man-made lake, not many cash customers showed up. I could never understand why. Almost every chimp that had ever bitten Johnny Weismuller was working there, and there were also a few chimps that *he* had bitten, too. The last I heard, Monkey Island was still there, but the monkeys were long gone. Mostly they had been adopted by nearsighted movie stars who couldn't have any of their own.

As I sat there in the twilight of that beautiful, soft fall night, breathing in the fresh, clean country air, I didn't see how I could leave. But I didn't see how I could stay, either. We had only forty dollars in the bank.

We left Bucks County the next day. I didn't even get a chance to say goodbye to Mr. Ulm. I called but he was out. Looking for Charlie again. I heard the bloodhounds faintly as we drove away. They sounded happy.

In California, we leased a house at Trancas Beach, which is about twelve miles north of Malibu. There were only three houses on this beautiful white sand beach, and we lived in between a movie director, Archie Mayo, and the now combination lady-and-houri actress, Deborah Kerr. Miss Kerr, at the time was married to Tony Somebody-or-Other who never came out of the house, was expecting a baby—apparently at any moment. Every day for nearly five months straight, we sat side by side in the sand in front of our houses, not saying a word. I had been taught that the lady must speak first, so I waited. But she didn't speak, and she didn't have the baby. Finally, I could stand it no longer, so I said, "Miss Kerr—when in the hell are you going to have the baby?" And she said, "*What* baby? This is a muu-muu, and my husband told me you were a deaf mute!"

The Skelton show turned out to be a smash. This was his first year in television, and he lived up to all the predictions that everybody in and out of the business had made. Red won an "Emmy" for that first year, and everybody was ecstatic. I should have been happy too, but I wasn't. Things were falling apart on the home front. I don't know what it was. Maybe the beach was too lonely. Maybe I was too lonely. I still don't know. Then one day, for no reason at all, I bought a C-type Jaguar, which is built purely for racing. My wife warned me: if I ever raced it, she'd leave me. I raced it. She left me.

CHAPTER 18

Thrills, Chills, Spills, and Bills

ONE NIGHT LAST YEAR, while I was doing my act at the Slate Brothers' night club in Hollywood, my former racing mechanic, a wonderful Englishman named Joe Thrall, was in the audience, and I wanted to introduce him in a rather serious and more or less dramatic manner. I wanted to say, "In automobile racing you have to depend on three things: God. Yourself. And your mechanic." And then I would introduce Joe. As it turned out, I got as far as, "In automobile racing you have to depend on three things: God. Yourself——." At that moment someone at the back of the room piped up with, "And Lance Reventlow!" Well, of course it got a scream from the audience, but it sure crumbed up my big dramatic scene.

Automobile racing could never take the place of a happy home, but in my case it helped ease the pain. I started racing (sports cars) before I had ever seen a race. I think if I had, I might have changed my mind. My first race was at the Torrey Pines course, near San Diego, California. Torrey Pines really wasn't the kind of a course for a beginner. In fact, it was one of the most dangerous racecourses in the country. Two people were killed my first day of racing. One, an electrician fixing the communications system alongside the track, was run down by a wild motorcycle (they were having motorcycle races that same day), and the second, a girl, jello-ed her car and herself into a cement wall, in the first turn of the women's race. This didn't bother me. I felt like everybody else in the world feels: accidents always happen to the other guy. Not that I wasn't scared to death, sitting on the starting grid, waiting for the green flag to be dropped. I was very scared, but as soon as the race started, I was too busy to be scared. Also, I tried to remember all the things that other race drivers had told me. The main thing, they had told me, was to take it easy. Lay back and watch the good drivers. I didn't do anything but this, in that first race, and it's a very good system. Little by little, I got bolder (in other races), until I could hold my own with almost everybody except the real greats, like Phil Hill, Richie Ginther, Carrol Shelby, Masten Gregory, Briggs Cunningham and a few others. All in all, I picked up about thirty trophies, and one year (1955) I was No. 10 in the national ratings.

After a time, I graduated to a D-type Jaguar, which is an extremely fast, if somewhat unmanageable, car, until the good Joe Thrall had tamed it with sway bars, locked rear ends and other stabilizing influences. As to the speed of my D-Jag, I had been clocked, unbeknownst to me, at 167.5

miles per hour on an extra long straightaway at Palm Springs. What I mean when I say unbeknownst to me, is that every racing car has a speedometer, but most drivers rarely, if ever, look at it. The tachometer is the thing to watch, to prevent over-revving your engine. Between 5800 RPM and 6000 RPM was the safe amount of revolutions for the D-Jag, which means that when you start off in first gear you step on the accelerator until the tachometer reads about 5900 RPM, then you shift into second gear. The tachometer drops way down and you step on the accelerator until the tachometer hits 5900 RPM again. Then you continue this process on up until you're in fourth gear (or fifth gear in certain types of Ferraris). When you hit top gear you watch the tachometer to make sure you don't go over 5900 RPM or whatever the danger point is in the car you're driving.

At 167 miles per hour you have very little control of the car, or so it seems. The car itself feels like it's taking off in all directions from under you. The slightest bump, or puddle of water, or gust of wind all but wrenches the steering wheel out of your hands, and a bug splattering against the windscreen makes a sound like a pistol shot. But anybody can drive a car at 167 miles an hour down a straight stretch of comparatively level road. The trick is to slow it down in time to go around a right angle corner at 25 miles an hour. This takes skill, and this is *when* and *where* races are *won* and *lost*. You have to go as deep into a corner as is safely possible in fourth gear. Which means as close to the corner as possible. Then you have to shift from fourth to third to second quickly. The quicker, the better, if you want to be anywhere near the leaders. If you are only one tenth of a second slower in shifting than the guy in front of you on each corner of, say, a thirteen-corner course in a one hundred lap race, you'll be going around the course one and three-tenths seconds *slower* than he is for *each* lap. In other words, at the end of the race you'll be two minutes and ten seconds or approximately four miles behind him. Very statistical, I realize, but bear with me. This is the first time *I've* figured this thing out *myself*. No wonder Phil Hill was always four miles ahead of me!

Most racecourses try to have what they call "escape roads" at the end of long straightaways, for those who don't shift down in time to go around a 25-mile-an-hour right-angle corner. But even with these escape roads, you have to make up your mind instantly that you can't make the corner. Then you just keep going straight until you're able to stop your car, turn around and come back to the course. One thing I learned early in racing was that if you start any act at all, follow through until it is completed. In other words, if you commit yourself, go through with it. Changing your mind in the middle of an act can be fatal—for example, if you start to turn a corner, then change your mind and decide to take the escape road. If you're going fast enough, your car will start to spin wildly, which isn't too bad if you are on an airport course. There will be plenty of room to spin, and the other drivers can avoid running into you, but if you're driving a narrow *road* course, you're bound to get clobbered by other cars and/or crash into a tree or a ditch or a rock or whatever Kismet has planned for you. Also, when you make an instant decision, it should be the right one. To illustrate, Ernie McAfee, at the last turn at Pebble Beach (Calif.), apparently missed a gearshift, shifting down from third to second, and his car was running free, in neutral, and too fast to make the right-angle turn. Ernie, instead of running forward and down the escape road, hit his brakes, probably a little harder than he should have, so he could make the turn. They locked, and the car immediately upended into a large pine tree, and Ernie was killed. He had made an instant decision, but it was the wrong one.

I had a few mishaps during my four years of racing, none of them serious. The day after the Sports Car Club of America made it mandatory that you must carry a fire extinguisher in the cockpit of your car, I was driving round a rather fast bend, during a race at Salt Lake City, when the fire extinguisher exploded from the heat of the exhaust pipe, and the CO_2 instantly gassed me unconscious. The car wandered off the course and through the fields and gradually slowed to a stop.

Another time, at Torrey Pines, I hit an oil slick, immediately lost all control of the car, and it flipped over, luckily landing on top of some hay bales which prevented the car from landing on top of *me*. After the car stopped teetering, I flipped open my safety belt, dropped to the ground, crawled out and was helped into a waiting ambulance. This whole thing was a great annoyance to the rest of the guys in the race, because under the caution flag they all had to slow down and more or less *line up* in back of the ambulance as it drove around the whole course back to the pits. I sat up and waved at them from the ambulance, but nobody waved back. The ambulance attendants gave me an antishock pill and told me to take it easy.

Contrary to a bio which was put out last year by my public relations expert, I didn't give up racing after this. I liked *it* and the people in it too much. I *did* give it up about three years later, when I left California and came back to New York to write the Jack Paar *Tonight* show. To race cars, and really be good at it, takes an awful lot of time. Most races are on weekends, which means, if you are driving to an event, pulling your race car on a trailer, you have to leave on a Thursday or a Friday, depending on how far it is, then drive the same distance back, cutting your workaday week down to about two days, which doesn't thrill most employers. Besides the time consumed, the expense is enormous. A good race car costs from ten to twenty thousand dollars. Every race will cost on the average of five to seven hundred dollars, counting setting up the car, new tires, transportation and living expenses for yourself and your mechanic. Twice I had the Flying Tigers air freight fly cars for me, once from L.A. to Chicago, and once from L.A. to Seattle. I'm *still* paying *them*. But it was worth it— I picked up a couple of dandy trophies that must be worth all of seven dollars each.

CHAPTER **19**

The Day That Jimmy Dean Died

JIMMY DEAN was not a friend of mine, but I did know him slightly, from his short career in sports car racing. Jimmy drove in exactly two races: one, for beginners, at Palm Springs, which he won, and the other at Bakersfield (Calif.), in which his car conked out and he didn't finish. I saw him after this race, and he was almost tearful because of his bad luck, which struck me, at the time, as a little peculiar, because the car conked out due to a mechanical defect. It was nothing Jimmy had done, but he seemed to be blaming himself anyway.

The next time I saw Jimmy was on the morning of the day he was to die. A bunch of us met at Jack McAfee's. Jack was a very good race driver who had a beautiful sister and a garage and salesroom on Ventura Boulevard in the San Fernando Valley. We were all leaving that morning to drive to Salinas for the races that weekend. Jimmy Dean was there with his German mechanic, Rolf Weurtheric. Jimmy had just bought a new Porsche Spyder and was going to *drive* it to Salinas just to get used to handling it a little better. I remember Rolf turning down a ride with Johnny Porter—another Porsche Spyder driver, who was towing his car up to Salinas—in order to stay with Dean, in case of any mechanical difficulties on the way. After a cup of coffee, most of us took off, because it was quite a long drive to Salinas, and towing a car slowed you down quite a bit. When we left, Jimmy was leaning up against a greasy bench, sipping his coffee and looking off into space.

We didn't travel as a caravan, and soon we lost track of each other. Besides, we all had our favorite routes to Salinas. Some time after noon, and north of Bakersfield, I turned off Highway 99 onto 466 which cut over from the inland to the coast route at Paso Robles. Highway 466 was quite narrow, but there was very little traffic, so it was easy driving. I didn't see any of the others, who had left when I did, but Jimmy and Rolf passed me later, tooting as they passed. After a while, the road started winding up into some small hills, then down again through more small hills. The road was extremely narrow here, and I was relieved finally to see the end of the hills and a nice long stretch of straight road downhill ahead of me, but almost immediately I became aware of a car in the middle of the road at the bottom of the hill. The front end of the car was toward me, and its hood was sprung open. When I got closer, I saw an ambulance pulling away, and a police car standing at one side of the road. On the other side of the road, in a wide ditch there was a small greyish-colored car upside down and smashed practically flat. I stopped and asked the cop, who was the only person in sight, what had happened, and he said some guy coming down the hill had clipped this other car (the one with the hood up) and had gone out of control and landed in the ditch. That's *all* he'd tell me, and, truthfully, it's all I wanted to know. I'm not an accident chaser usually, and especially when I'm driving to a race meet.

A little later, I stopped in Paso Robles for coffee (it was dark now) when some fat dame bounced into this little hamburger stand, sat down beside me and said: "That your car outside? You gonna race it in Salinas?" I said "Yes," twice. Then she said, "Ya hear it on the radio? Some movie actor got killed in a car." She didn't know his name, or where it had happened, but I knew right away that it was Jimmy Dean, and where it had happened.

Vampira, a friend of his, and when she felt like it, a friend of mine, summed it up by saying: "It was the first time Jimmy ever trusted anybody, and *this* is what happens." She was referring to the fact that the car Dean's car had *barely touched* made a left turn directly in front of him when, according to Rolf, who was terribly mangled but alive, Jimmy expected the other car to wait until he had gone by, before turning. There was *nothing* to obscure the view on both sides of the road for hundreds of yards. It looked to me as though the man who made the turn in front of Dean's car couldn't help seeing him coming and how close he was, but took a chance and turned anyway. It was senseless and stupid.

And just in passing, such a righteous stink was raised

over Dean's having been given a ticket for speeding in Bakersfield a couple of hours before—for the record—in Bakersfield, if you drive a *sports car* they'll give you a ticket for *backing up!*

CHAPTER 20

Only One Bluebird To A Customer

AT THE TIME I was doing all this car racing I lived in Holly-wood at a place called the "Sweetzer-Lanai." It was called the "Sweetzer" because it was located on Sweetzer Avenue, and "Lanai" because Sol Lanai was one of the owners. At the risk of sounding like Mary Martin on benzedrine, I'd like to say that this was a *very, very* happy time in my life.

It was a happy time because of the people who lived in this lush, palm-tree-infested rookery. They were wonderful people, so far as I knew. Maybe it was just the indirect lighting, but I don't think so. Mitzi Gaynor lived there with her husband. Their front door mat said "Welcome—Archie and Leota." Eve Arden lived there with her husband. Their front doormat didn't say anything. Vic Tanny lived there with his muscles. He didn't have a front door mat, but he had firebreaks shaved on his chest that spelled out "Hi,

Neighbor." Some of the other nice people who lived there were Jack Rose, an old friend and a movie producer at Paramount; Jimmy Saphier, another old friend and Bob Hope's manager; Sam (I never knew his last name), a very nice but mysterious guy who kept time by girls who visited him every hour on the hour. Then there was Brenda, a beautiful little blonde girl, who drove a green Austin-Healey into the garage about three a.m. every morning. She never failed to rev the engine up as high as it would go before she turned off the key. This blew the carbon off the spark plugs, and also moved my bed a couple of inches off the floor, because my apartment was right over her garage stall. Then of course, there were a few other actors and actresses who lived in the building. Some of them were married to each other. Occasionally. There were also a few squares living there—the kind of people who get up and go to work at the same time every day—you know, non-conformists. All in all, it was a gay group, and I use the word "gay" in its old-fashioned sense. If anyone was having a party, you were invited automatically. Actually, if you were having a party, you couldn't very well not invite everybody, because the Sweetzer-Lanai was only a two-story building built around a lovely swimming pool, and every apartment opened onto the swimming pool area, and if there was a party going on you were *right there* anyway; that's how you were automatically invited.

In the old days in Hollywood, there was an apartment hotel similar to the Sweetzer-Lanai on Sunset Boulevard, called the Garden of Allah, where such great pranksters as Robert Benchley, Charlie Butterworth, Gene Fowler, Ben Hecht and others took turns at shoving each other into the swimming pool, which of course, I have no doubt, was great fun—but then it always has been. I guess. At the Sweetzer-Lanai nobody pushed nobody into the swimming pool, but we still had a ball. Arthur, the guy in the apartment next to me, had the loudest hi-fi set west of the Mississippi, and a large collection of LP frog sounds. These frog sounds had been recorded in the Louisiana swamps by some nature nut, and they sounded just like frogs in a Louisiana swamp, when he kept the sound level where it was supposed to be, but if he turned the amplifier up as high as it would go, they'd sound like the invasion of Normandy and the sound track from *Ben-Hur* combined.

Usually about two o'clock in the morning (one hour before the blonde with the Austin-Healey came home) he would put on one of these recordings, and gradually turn up the gain. By the time the sound had reached its earth-shattering peak, the manager, Mrs. Billingsley, would be letting herself into Arthur's apartment with her pass key. The minute he saw the door knob move he'd snap off hi-fi, snatch up a Gideon Bible, a gift, he said, from Conrad Hilton, and be deeply engrossed in the twenty-third Psalm as she entered. Then he would look up at her and say, "And *you*, Beautiful Lady—where will *you* spend eternity?"

Mitzi Gaynor, who was married to Jack Bean, lived upstairs, and Mitzi sunned herself every day at the pool in a bikini. As I said before, every apartment faced the pool, and it was very tough to keep your mind on your work and Mitzi at the same time, but somehow I managed to. Jack and Mitzi were very happy with each other, which annoyed me no end. I tried to break the whole thing up with sly innuendos to both of them. When Mitzi was at the pool, I used to slither up to her and drop remarks like, "I saw Jack at lunch today. He was getting loaded with Vilma Banky." Then when Jack would come home from work, I'd grab him before he went upstairs, and say, "Jack, the husband is always the *last* to *know*." And when he'd say, "Know what?" I'd say, "Stan Laurel was over here today, and he and Mitzi . . ." Then I'd sort of trail off and leave it at that. These tactics never seemed to work, and these two trouble-makers are *still* happy with each other.

Vic Tanny, who was well on his way to being a trillion-aire through his swing and sweat parlors, was a nice, easy-going and gentle man, but he could squeeze your head flat with his pinkies—although I only saw him do this *once*. (To some guy who had just spent three hundred dollars learning karaté.) The gardener who took care of the jungle of tropical plantings in and around the Sweetzer-Lanai was a Mexican. By all the rules to be a gardener in California he should have been Japanese, but somebody had goofed. I first met him when he knocked at my door and said, "*Buenas tardes, Señor.* I water the plants. Every day I water the plants." Then after a pause he said, "Some days I water the plants twice." I said, "Why do you water the plants twice?" and he said, "Please do not try to confuse me, Señor. I am but a poor peon you gotta hi-fi?" I said, "Yes." Then he said, "You play my record?" I said, "No." There was another long pause, then he said, "You wanna know why some days I water the plants twice?" I said, "No." Then he reached in under his shirt and pulled out a grimy LP album and handed it to me. I looked at the cover for a moment then I handed it back to him. He stared at me, incredulously. Tears started running down his well-grooved cheeks. Struggling for con-

117

trol, he said, "You don't like—Mickey Katz?" I couldn't stand it. "Come on in," I said.

Brenda, the little blonde who owned the Austin-Healey, was a woman of mystery to me—at *first*. Then one day I was in the garage when she came down, got into her car and started revving up the engine as usual. I told her she'd wreck the whole thing if she kept doing this. Then I carefully explained that the oil has to have a chance to get up on the cylinders before they can be revved up, etc. I don't know whether my explanation was technically correct, but that's the way I understand it. She listened to my whole lecture, then revved the engine up even higher and took off.

The next time I saw her she wasn't nearly so unfriendly. It was down in the garage again, and I had just driven in, in my brand-new shiny black Cadillac convertible. She asked me up for a drink and to meet her husband. This kind of arrangement left much to be desired, but I went. And I'm glad I did, because her husband was leaving the next day, I found out, for New York, to produce a play or something. And even later still, after a magnum of martinis, I found out that he *wasn't* her husband, and he *wasn't* going to New York to produce a play—he was going to *Acapulco* because he was on the lam.

I didn't see Brenda for a week or so, because I was out of town—racing. When I came back, I saw her almost immediately, because my car had been smashed up a bit, and I needed something to race at Hansen Dam, which was a new course in the San Fernando valley. Brenda didn't think much of me racing her car at Hansen Dam, and truthfully, *I* didn't like the idea of driving a production Austin-Healey. However, I won her over after I changed the inscription

118

on my ID bracelet in favor of her. I also signed an agreement to pay all damage that might be incurred to her car, plus the installation of a safety belt and a general overhaul of the car to get it into more or less "racing" condition. As it turned out, the changing of the ID inscription, the safety belt and the overhaul went for naught. Driving this car in the production car race was disastrous. Every time I touched the brakes, the car turned and broadslided down the track. The Hansen Dam race meeting was the first and the *last*. The course was extremely rough and excessively narrow. Some of the turns had room for only one car. This came as a complete surprise to me when I found myself in a turn with *two* other cars, and all three of us hurdled the hay bales and surprised about fifty spectators as we drove right into them. They all scrambled reluctantly out of the way, but I wound up between the back wheels of a large truck, without a scratch on *me;* however, the car, as they say, was totaled. I had to lend Brenda my Cadillac, while her car was being fixed, and she used it every night and with a different guy each time. One night, towards the end of our friendship (?), I lent her about twenty or thirty books on philosophy, psychology and psychiatry, which she said she was studying. She moved out the same night and I never saw her again. But I *fixed her*. I had the inscription on my ID bracelet erased.

One lovely June day—tragedy struck the Sweetzer-Lanai. It changed hands, and with the new ownership came a new manager, a Mrs. Rumson, who was more like a warden than a manager. She handled the tenants with all the charm of Eric Von Stroheim kicking a peasant to death. Her first act was to fire all the wonderful colored maids and to bring in her own group—from the "sick" branch of the Ku Klux Klan. The Mickey Katz-loving Mexican gardener was replaced by a student of atrophy, whose sole purpose in life was to explore the inside of his nose.

Things were quiet, but not for long. The third night of the reign of Mrs. Rumson turned out to be the hottest night we had ever had in Southern California, and some of us dared to use the swimming pool after *nine* o'clock. This brought out the Gestapo leader, screaming maniacally; her ceremonial gown (she'd just been killing a goat) was wet with froth, and she was so hysterical she had trouble making herself understood, but we finally gathered it was "everybody outa the pool!" Nobody moved "outa the pool," and nobody said anything. Finally, even Mrs. Rumson stopped yelling and just stood there dying in her living bra. This was too good an opportunity, I thought, so not quite under control, I climbed up the pool steps, walked over to her and said: "Mrs. Rumson—Why don't you go back to managing that Tia Juana crib and leave us alone!" This pleasantry earned me her undying hatred. From that moment on, my life at the Sweetzer-Lanai was nothing but turmoil. Turmoil, I might add, for both sides. This was real civil war. First, she practically cut off my maid service. They would make the bed, but that was about all. They refused, from that day on, to wash my dirty dishes, for which I had always tipped them well, since they were frightened to death of this Sweetzer-Lanai Fury. The next thing she did was have the zombie gardener bring everything of mine up from the storeroom and dump it in the middle of my living room. This made quite a dump, because it included, among other things, several spare racing tires and wheels, a stack of automobile tools, and three steamer trunks full of old income tax data. All this, of course, was done while I was out, and it made a nice surprise to come home to.

All I could think of, naturally, was retaliation. I started first with a large can of red poster paint. On my large picture window, which was filthy, I painted this legend: "This window has not been cleaned for one and a half years." The very next day it was cleaned, but only the side with the message on it. Down below, and across from my apartment, was the filter room for the swimming pool, and the noise from the filtering plant was very annoying. There was a small sign on the metal door: "Please keep this door closed." But I kept finding it *open* after Mrs. Rumson had declared war, so one day, when *she* was out, I welded the door shut and also painted in bright red the "Please keep this door closed" sign a little larger. Ten feet high and twenty feet long.

This didn't stop the Bride of Frankenstein. She poured Elmer's glue in my front door lock cylinder. I discovered this at eight o'clock one morning as I was coming home, after driving straight through from Fort Worth. I sent for a locksmith, and she sent for the Sheriff and tried to have me arrested for breaking and entering.

Finally, I had to admit that I was licked, and moved out, but not before repainting the whole apartment—with peanut butter.

CHAPTER 21

Never Goose A Rogue Elephant

EVERY ONCE IN A WHILE, when I discovered that I had one wife too many, or the Friendly Finance Company turned out to be just the opposite, I'd run for home, which at that time was Banning, California. Banning was a health-resort town, and the hot, dry desert air and the 2500-feet elevation were supposed to be very good for people with TB, asthma, arthritis, etc.

My parents seemed to be very happy in Banning. There were many people from all over the world living there, for health reasons, and they were extremely friendly people and also a cut above the average small-town intelligence. Mother was always very busy with this or that club, while Dad spent most of his days gardening. Gardening in the desert, of course, consisted mainly of trying to keep everything from dying of thirst—including yourself if you got a little too far from the house. And Dad was always at war with a large family of gophers who lived, and very well too, off of what he planted. Dad's favorite method of trying to discourage them was to shove a water hose down a gopher's hole—or maybe a better way to put it, down a gopher's residence. Then he would turn the water on full force and try to drown the little bastards. But the little bastards were a lot smarter than Dad. A gopher's residence has more secret escape exits than a three-dollar motel. In all the twelve years that Dad spent pouring water down gopher holes, I don't think there was even a single gopher who so much as got his *feet* wet. It was a good try, but what Dad didn't know was that they were the first "Untouchables."

I guess most normal mothers and fathers are pretty much alike in their feelings toward their children. No matter what you do, they're still on your side, but looking back, I certainly put my parents to the test a few times. One night I was driving, quite drunkenly, from Long Beach to Banning when suddenly I decided to take a short cut through some strange side streets somewhere around El Monte. I was barreling along about sixty or seventy, and everything was fine until I hit a deep, sharp dip in the road. Immediately, the car and I parted company. The car, a brand-new Ford roadster, fell in love with a telephone pole, and I was flung out and into the back of a milkman's truck. The milkman evidently smelt the alcohol fumes, and being a good guy took me to his home, and instead of calling the police, he called my mother. My mother drove the sixty or seventy miles all the way from Banning at three o'clock in the morning through a blinding rain and windstorm, and all this with-

123

out knowing quite what to expect when she got to the milkman's house.

Actually, there wasn't too much wrong with me. I had received quite a jolt in my belly from the steering wheel and quite a few cuts and bruises from the abrupt contact with the wooden boxes stacked in the milk truck. But just like all drunks, I landed limp and this saved me from anything more serious. On the way back to Banning, we got off the side of the road on the long stretch between Pomona and Colton and got stuck in the sand, and it took Mother two hours to dig us out. I was in no condition to help. I was sober but too bruised to walk, let alone excavate an impacted Pontiac. When we finally got to Banning, there was an air of restraint around the house, mostly from Dad, because although he had always approved of me, he did it secretly. When I first started in vaudeville, he used to sneak into the theatre to watch me, but I didn't find this out until years later.

What rallied us into being a family again was the statement of the dealer that I had bought my car from. He said it had no insurance on it and that I would have to pay for the car even if it was a total loss, and it was. The fact that in my contract with him there was a certain amount set aside for collision insurance he ignored completely. He evidently had pocketed the insurance money, that I had paid him, taking his chances that I would never have an accident, or if I did have one and the cost for repair was small he would pay it himself. At the time I was either too dumb or too poor—or both—to fight this crook. Anyhow, I didn't pay for the car, and the dealer's threat that I would never again be able to own a car in California was just empty words.

Some day I would like to walk into this dealer's again and give him something that he deserves—and I don't mean a belting. I want to give him a *trophy*—for *guts*. Imagine—a guy with a jail sentence hanging over him, for bunco or swindling or whatever the technical term is, *still* threatening the buncoed or swindled or whatever the technical term is for "pigeon." It would have to be a *large* trophy.

Banning was also a good town for getting rid of a hangover and a belly burn, and in no time I was out and around. My chief pleasure in Banning was hiking through the desert. To me the desert was a fascinating place. It was filled with many different kinds of cactus, which were covered with beautiful flowers at certain times of the year, and also the desert had plenty of wildlife, like horned toads, lizards, jackrabbits, coyotes, and many rattlesnakes—or, as the editor of *Downbeat* calls them— "noisy worms." I didn't see many coyotes, because they're mainly nocturnal, but the rattlesnakes were all over the place. People always want to know what a rattlesnake sounds like, but it's impossible to describe. All you can tell them is they'll know the sound when they hear it, and this is true. There's no mistaking it. But there's nothing to worry about if you *do* hear a rattler; he won't attack you. On the contrary, he'll get the hell away from you as fast as he can. And this is true of all wild things. There never has been a single *substantiated* instance of any wild animal *ever* attacking a human being—no matter how many television "adventure" movies you've seen. The *attacking* is always done by the brave "white" hunters, at the request of the "defenseless" natives to kill the "rogue" elephant who has been stepping on their rice paddies.

It is never explained why the "defenseless" natives, who

are usually armed to the teeth with the latest automatic weapons and who certainly know the country a helluva lot better than these Abercrombie & Fitch tourists, don't knock off the rogue themselves. Maybe it's because they don't have movie cameras. Of course, wild animals *can* be dangerous, but only if provoked, so if you happen to be in big game country, and you want to keep out of trouble, remember; never goose a rogue elephant. Or for that matter, a nervous gun-bearer.

It was in Banning that I first noticed segregation. At the Banning movie theatre the Indians had to sit on the right side of the house, and the whites sat on the other. The Indians had all the best of this deal, because the Banning theatre's sound system was faulty. On the right side it was perfect; on the other side you couldn't hear anything. When there was a really *good* picture there used to be an awful lot of honorary Indians. And the Indians didn't seem to mind. Actually, there weren't enough of them to object too strenuously. The Banning Indians were of the Mission tribe, and they didn't have too much on the ball to begin with, but now they really were a sorry lot and they had a *lousy* reservation. No oil, no gas, no uranium, no nothing; actually, they were lucky they had Indians.

The Indians, in order to make a few dollars, used to sell firewood to the townspeople. The firewood was ten dollars a cord, but for some reason or other they never delivered a full cord. They'd fill up the backs of their old jalopies with wood, and because it was never cut to any particular length, it was impossible to figure a full cord anyway, so people would just guess at what percentage of a cord they had brought, and pay them for that. Although once, an Indian *did* bring a full cord to our next-door neighbor, Mr. Ralph Fell. Mr. Fell, only partially recovered from the shock, refused to pay the Indian the full price of ten dollars, because he still didn't believe what he saw. The Indian, a brave named Red Mud, blew the whistle on Mr. Fell, and the first thing Banning knew, it was involved in the very last of the Indian wars. The war was a draw. The convalescents of Banning were no match for the doddering descendants of Geronimo—and vice-versa. Mr. Fell finally paid the ten dollars, and a treaty was signed, and all was quiet once again.

From then on the Mission Indians lived on their reservation in the Morongo Valley, and were peaceable enough, except once when an Indian agent who represented the Great White Father in Washington interrupted one of their religious ceremonies and promptly got himself shot right between the eyes. The agent, who knew better than to interrupt any Indian religious ceremony, was trespassing, but nevertheless the Indian who killed him was given a life sentence, which for an Indian meant about six years. That's about as long as an Indian can live in jail.

Banning, in the late eighteen hundreds, had been a station on the old Butterfield stage line. Most of the great heroes and villains of the West had passed through town at one time or another; Billy the Kid, the James boys, the Dalton gang, Bat Masterson, Wyatt Earp and many others had all refreshed and/or relieved themselves in Banning, on their way to or from Los Angeles. They still do, as a matter of fact; Banning is on the main road from Hollywood to Palm Springs.

Palm Springs is quite different from Banning, although it's in the same desert. Palm Springs is a beautiful place, and it's made out of neon. It's situated in the shadow of snow-covered Mount San Jacinto and would be below sea level if it weren't for the prices. When I first discovered the place there was nothing much there except a lovely old hotel, the Desert Inn, which is still there. But Palm Springs itself has changed tremendously. Hundreds of developments have sprung up on all sides. The houses in these developments come as a kit and are glued together. Of course, if you don't follow the instruction sheet carefully you may wind up with a Polaris sub, which would have a helluva time trying to crash-dive in the sand.

Palm Springs has Indians, too, but they're much better off than the Banning Indians. The Palm Springs Indians own most of this valuable desert resort land. Another foul-up of our Washington Indian treaty bureau. First Oklahoma—then this! But anyway, most of this land is leased to the whites, and is now covered with motels, hotels, restaurants, homes and "likker" stores. I don't think that the Indians are making what they should out of all this, but it's a lot better than standing along the road all day in the hot sun, selling Japanese Navaho Indian blankets to the tourists.

The Indians of Palm Springs, which is part of the Agua Caliente (Hot Water) reservation, also own some mud baths there. These mud baths are very hot and stink of sulfur, but for a small fee they make you feel like a new man —or a new woman—whatever your preference. These mud baths are covered by crude wooden shacks, and are extremely primitive, and the Indians so far have resisted any

My Hollywood office-studio where I wrote scripts and also took nude photos and had a cold most of the time

This could *have been a helluva lot* shorter *book*
(Torrey Pines, California, 1956)

A

C

B

D

E

F

ABOVE: *Me and a talking dog on the Paar show. This dog had only a two-word vocabulary. This picture was taken just after he'd said them.* (1958)

BELOW: "My *saber is bent, too*" ('21' Club, 1960)

"Jack Douglas is to a drum what the guillotine was to Marie Antoinette."—MITCH MILLER

Just look in the yellow pages of your phone book under 'Girls—Geisha'
(The Teahouse of the August Moon—Chicago, 1961)

私達は天国に居る様な夏休サ！

Southhampton Motel

attempts to improve them in any way. As one old brave put it to the head of the Palm Springs Chamber of Commerce, who was trying to get him to police up the area, "Forget it, Sweetie—a mud bath is not a tidy thing."

CHAPTER 22

With The Peace Corps In Sodom and Gomorrah

I STAYED IN HOLLYWOOD after my Dunkirk at the Sweetzer-Lanai, and moved up the street to the Sunset-Lanai. They'd heard all about me at the Sunset-Lanai. Mrs. Rumson had sent out an all-points bulletin, but they welcomed me anyway. I don't really know why except that in the manager's apartment I noticed a petit point seat cover on a chair with the motto: "There's no such thing as a bad boy," signed "Mrs. Dillinger." I also noticed some wires running down the leg of the chair to the nearest wall socket. But I didn't ask any questions and neither did they. The Sunset-Lanai was a little more sedate than the Sweetzer-Lanai. Among the residents were the mild-mannered Mr. Anthony of radio fame. He was a great favorite and made a fortune solving marital problems on the air. Remember *"No names,* please!"? Mr. Anthony had recently solved one of his own marital problems, and on the days that he mailed his alimony check we stayed out of his way. No names indeed! Seaman Jacobs, a very good comedy writer, lived two doors from me. Seaman *had* been married to Margie Hart, one of the strip-tease immortals. When they were married and lived in the valley, they had a wonderful little toy French poodle who used to perform at parties. Someone would throw a handful of change on the floor, then Seaman would tell the dog to pick up the smallest coin, which the dog would do. Also on command, this clever little mutt would pick up the largest coin. Margie wasn't so cooperative. She wouldn't do anything on command. Not at parties, anyway.

During this period I was at loose ends. I helped write a TV spectacular for Phil Harris, during the rehearsal of which, the director stamped his foot on the floor one day and screamed, "Oh *why* does everybody here *hate me?"* It took some time to compile, but before the show went on, we gave him a list. After that, Marvin Fisher and I wrote one episode of a new series for Eve Arden. The series, apparently, didn't turn out to be another "Our Miss Brooks" because I've never met anyone who has ever seen it. Including Eve Arden. Also about this time, I wrote three plays. One about a writer who sells his soul to the devil. Another about a trumpet player who sells his soul to the devil. And another about a scientist who sells his soul to the devil. And still another about a devil who is overstocked. One day during my obsession with the Prince of Darkness, I was driving down Sunset Boulevard when I spotted an extremely attractive girl in a white T-bird. She sort of half smiled so I took down her license number. Later through the license number I found out her name and where she lived, and sent her two dozen long stemmed red roses with a note on my stationery: "Although we may never meet, I want you to know I think you are very beautiful." The very next day I got a note back: "Alma wants me to thank you for the roses, and to tell you she thinks you are very beautiful, too," signed "Mickey Cohen."

After a couple of weeks of uneasy living I got back to writing. Eddie Fisher asked me to write a night club act for Brown and Beasley, a comedy team that he had great faith in. Eddie thought they'd be another Martin and Lewis. And it worked out that way, too. Just about the time that Martin and Lewis split up, Brown and Beasley did the same. Nobody thought that either one of them would make it on their own, but they were wrong. Brown is now the best bartender in Hollywood, and Beasley is his best customer. Or maybe it's the other way around.

I also wrote some night club material for Sue Carson, a clever young comedienne; Ann Sothern of "Maisie" fame; and Betty Hutton. And I promised each of them that I would be there for moral support and any script changes that might be needed on their respective opening nights. I should never have promised this because their respective opening nights turned out to be the *same* night. But with me a promise is a promise so I had to figure a way to be in Palm Springs, Lake Tahoe and Las Vegas simultaneously or have a very good reason why I couldn't be. I just couldn't let Sue or Ann or Betty think I was unreliable, so on opening night I sent each of them a ransom note. None of them ever came across with the five thousand dollars in small unmarked bills, but it got me off the hook.

I finally *did* see Betty Hutton's act. I had driven up to Las Vegas one New Year's Eve to be with a loved one, and Betty was playing at the Sands Hotel. I thought she did a great show. When I went back to her dressing room to congratulate her she looked like she'd just lost her whole family in a train wreck. She was inconsolable because there had been some restiveness in the audience while she was working. "What the hell, Betty," I said, "You've got to expect a little of that—it's New Year's Eve." And actually, the audience had been *very* attentive. But this didn't cut any ice with Betty. She thought somebody out there didn't like her, and her heart was broken. And when I said, "Come on and have a drink and forget it," she really fell apart. "How can I *forget* it," she moaned, "It's my *whole life!*" Well, Betty *is* quite dedicated, but I'm sure she knows that there's no such thing as a perfect audience—except maybe—at a lynching.

Somewhere along about this time, I was approached by my old friend Spike Jones to do some comedy material for a television series he was planning. Spike, who looks like he's lived on nothing but Metrecal since babyhood, wanted to do a satire on the old Kay Kayser "Kollege of Musical Knowledge" with Spike doing Kay's part. Kay had long since retired to his native North Carolina, which he owns. But, as it turned out, Spike and I agreed on everything except what was funny. This led to a trial separation, which is still in effect.

Jack Carson, for whom I had written a radio series, now wanted a night club act. I wrote one for him, and knowing his appetite for risqué material was a little on the voracious side, I wrote what I thought was a rather spicy act. Little did I know how spicy it was. I drove up to the Riverside Hotel in Reno the night he broke it in. With the lovely Connie Towers working as his foil, Carson did one of the most unscoured night club acts I have ever seen. And it was all written by *me*. It *was* risqué material, but with the Carson grimaces and gestures it had become positively pornographic. Alongside of Carson's act the Rape of the Sabines would have looked like an episode from "Lassie." And to top the evening off, he introduced me and made me stand up and take a bow. The author! I expected the vigilantes at any moment but I needn't have worried. The audience loved every minute of it, and later Carson was picked as Reno's entertainment man-of-the-year for which he was given a statuette, called the "Harold" which is sort of a crap shooter's "Oscar."

Driving back from Reno I got yelled at by an airplane. It's true—they've got planes with loudspeakers underneath and they hover over you as you're driving and yell things like "What's your hurry, Old Buddy? Slow up a little—and live!" Just when you think it's some kind of nutty safety campaign, some girl who sounds like a combination of Tokyo Rose and Salomé gets on and says, with a spermily quivering voice that echoes all over the valley, "Yeah, what's your hurry, Baby? Turn around and come back to Reno. You might get lucky. Whaddya say, Baby. Why doncha turn around? Huh, Baby?" In turning around, I hit a tree.

Not long after I came back from Reno, where I didn't get lucky the second time either, I received a phone call from my perennial employer, Jack Paar. He wanted to know whether I would come to New York and write the *Tonight* show, which he was taking over in July. The money was B-okay, and even though it meant leaving California at an inopportune time, I had just put twenty dollars down on a burial plot at Disneyland, I said yes.

CHAPTER 23

To The Barricades!

WHEN I FIRST MET Jack Paar, he had just left the army. It was right after the war finished, and Jack had given his word he wouldn't leave until it was over. When we met he had just started a new career in show business, which in Paar's case was sort of a continuation of the war. Paar had been selected by Jack Benny to be his summer radio show replacement. Immediately, he had several feuds going: one feud with his writers, one with Jack Hellman, the *Variety* critic, and one with Fred Allen. The first feud was terminated by the writers themselves; they left him. In all the years that have passed since then, I have never been able to find out from Paar or the writers, one of whom is a friend of mine, what the feud was all about. The second feud, with Jack Hellman, started, I presume, when Hellman's criticism of the show bruised Paar some way or another. Paar called me on the phone, read a letter that he had written in answer to Hellman, asking my advice as to whether he should send the letter or not. After hearing the letter,

I suggested it shouldn't be sent. "Too late," said Jack merrily. "I've already sent it!" The feud with Fred Allen was started by Allen himself on his radio show when he called Paar "the male Joan Davis"—a mildly *funny* aspersion, but nevertheless, an aspersion. Paar immediately retaliated in kind. This feud was relatively short-lived. After about three weeks Fred Allen stopped sniping at Paar, and in the opinion of many, this was none too soon. The sniper had run out of ammunition early in the game, and the snipee had sniped back with much heavier ammunition. Allen retired from the game, if not in confusion, at least in a puzzlement.

It was some time during all this that Jack had asked me to write his show, although I don't think he hired me for my writing. I think it was because he admired me for *my* feuds, and I had some dandies going! One was with General Motors and a local Buick Dealer, over the spark plugs in a 1940 or '41 Buick. The spark plugs had been an experiment (with Buick) and hadn't worked out too well, and the local dealer was supposed to change the engine head so it would accommodate larger spark plugs—for free. He changed the engine head all right, but he tried to charge me for it. This led to several sharp skirmishes and wound up with me calling Mr. Alfred P. Sloan, the president of General Motors. Mr. Sloan was most understanding and promised immediate action. True to his word, within the week, the local Buick dealer was back in Florida, selling two and one-half-acre plots of choice residential land—in the Everglades. Another hassle I was having was with the Los Angeles Light and Power Company, over a $2700 electric light bill—for one month. I thought it was a bit stiff. I tried to get them to send the bill to Mr. Hearst, at San Simeon

(I'm sure that's where it belonged), but they would have no part of this sensible suggestion. As a consequence, I spent many a long hour with the Los Angeles city attorney. Finally, they gave me the choice of paying the bill or having the electricity turned off. I said, "Go ahead, turn it off." This surprised them. They countered with, "You pay half the bill and we'll turn off only half the electricity." This sounded like a good deal, so we shook hands, and I went home wondering how they were going to do it. That night I found out. They just cut the power in half. A fifty-watt bulb now became twenty-five. A five hundred degree electric oven now became two-fifty. A thirty-three and a third record player now played at sixteen and four-sixths. Maria Callas sounded like a drunken Amos and Andy. The Los Angeles Light and Power Company had really slowed us down. But did they break our spirit? Yes. About two weeks later I paid the bill and charged it off to experience, which started *another feud*—with the Internal Revenue people.

Another, but lesser, feud on my ever-growing list was with the Los Angeles Water Company, over an inadvertently padded bill. When the truth came out, the meter reader stated a bush had grown over the meter, and he didn't want to get down on his hands and knees to read it, so he had just guessed at the amount of water consumed—and *this* in a community where water costs more than vodka.

My other feuds were more or less small-time. One was with Mayor Bowron, the L.A. mayor, over some minor matter, like I didn't want a freeway going through my backyard. I thought it conflicted with the hundred-foot steel high-tension towers that were already going through my backyard. I had one rather dangerous feud in operation at the time—dangerous physically. This was with a neighbor whose right hand consisted of only a hook, and several times he had ambushed me at the mailbox, because of my trombone playing at all hours of the night. He never quite hooked me, with his hook, but only because in those days I could move like Manolete, and frequently had to.

Another feud I've nurtured through the years is with Jack Douglas. The fake Jack Douglas. There is one, you know. He's the producer of television adventure films. The fake Jack Douglas is a man who entered the entertainment field quite some time after I did, and why he didn't choose to use his *own* name, which is Pablo Lipshitz or Mervin Tooze or something like that, I've never been able to find out. Or why he doesn't call himself Fabian?—or Leonard Bernstein?—or Doctor Albert Schweitzer? They're all pretty good names, and they might help me to sell a lot more home movies—I mean, "adventure" films. He's used my name so long now that he has become indignant over *my* using it. A couple of years ago he sent a wire to Leo Guild of the trade paper, *The Hollywood Reporter*, stating that he wanted *everyone* to *know* that he wasn't Jack Douglas, the *writer*. To which Leo replied, in his column, "And aren't you *sorry?*" I'm kinda sorry, too, now that I think about it. Maybe I'd be happier if *my* name was Mervin Tooze or Pablo Lipshitz.

After Jack Paar and I had consolidated our feuds, I went to work on his radio program. It was a good program, and it was renewed for another thirteen weeks after the initial summer season. It was still a good program, but it ended rather abruptly, I thought, the night Jack sang.

After this, I wrote for Paar on whatever program he was on, and he was on quite a few, and all through the years he picked up loyal fans on the way. When I say loyal fans, I don't mean the cretins who crawl around outside Sardi's in New York or the Brown Derby in Hollywood, clutching drool-covered autograph books in their claws, and yelling when you come out: "Are *you* anybody?" I always say, "No, but I once pissed on Edna May Oliver's fur coat." (I thought it was a mink urinal). This makes me *somebody*, and I get to sign every time!

Paar's fans have been accumulated over the years. They watch, listen and enjoy, and they don't write letters. Of course, nowadays, there are thousands of people who say they don't watch Paar any more. I meet some of them every day. They always say, when they spot Reiko and me, "We see you every night on television!" Then in the next breath they tell you they don't watch Paar any more. I know it would be fruitless to say, "How do you avoid seeing Paar while you're watching Reiko and me on television *every night?*" Maybe they all wear eye patches. Who knows?

The *Tonight* show started at the end of July, 1957. Almost everyone "in the industry" spoke of the first show as "almost a disaster," "Paar was extremely nervous," "the whole thing was chaotic." It wasn't. It was funny as hell. It's still chaotic, Paar is still nervous, and he still keeps the show on the edge of disaster—the way Fangio did when he was winning his many world auto racing championships. If all this sounds like a defense of Jack Paar, it is. And it's pretty silly. Why am I helping St. George, when it's the dragon that's in trouble?

The *Tonight* show was first broadcast from the Hudson Theatre on West 44th Street. It was a wonderful old smelly theatre, and had been the home of many Broadway hits and the home grounds of past Broadway greats, like George M. Cohan, who was the Paul Anka of his day. Paar didn't care for the Hudson Theatre much. It was just a little bit too untidy for him. And it really was untidy—actually, "dirty" would be a better word—but it had the "feel" of theatre, and it was in a district reeking with theatrical atmosphere. Eugene O'Neill had been born in a drugstore around the corner at 43rd and Broadway. There was a bronze plaque telling all about it, in front of the store. The Lambs Club was across the way, and I used to get a kick out of seeing some of the famous actors come and go—some of them having a bit of trouble negotiating the steps, for one reason or other. George Jean Nathan lived up the street in a Mansfield Hotel penthouse. His wife, Julie Haydon, lived in another apartment in the same hotel, a strange arrangement unless you think about it for a moment. The Algonquin Hotel was a block away from the Hudson Theatre, and, of course, had been world-famous for its Round Table, frequented by the wits of the time. What the hell ever happened to *them?* Paar had a suite at the Algonquin, which he used strictly as an office. He's that kind of a guy. There was another fascinating institution a few doors away from the Hudson Theatre, the 123 Hotel. It was by far the most exciting hotel in the world. Hardly a night went by without a shooting, a gouging, a machete massaging or a fire axe chopping bee. The 123's tenants were a fairly nervous group

—especially about women, because apparently most of the fights were over women. Some nights, from the bloody reports in the morning papers, it seemed they had all wanted the same one. At the same time.

My financial advisor had a place near the Hudson Theatre. His name was Andy, and he was Greek, and he owned a restaurant. He couldn't dance a step, but he was the Nick Darvas of 44th Street. His accent was pretty hard to understand, and I'm quite sure I bought the wrong stock more than once. For instance, Israel petroleum. This was one of Andy's tips, and for some strange reason Israel petroleum is located in Australia, and the way the stock acted after I bought it, I wish I had bought *Australian* petroleum and discovered that it was located in *Israel*. At least I could tell Jessel that I was doing my part.

Writing for Paar on the *Tonight* show was fun, but very confining. The show went on every night (Monday to Friday) at 11:15, and there was no taping it early then, or no "Best of Paar" on Fridays (which were re-runs of past shows). Speaking of this last, Reiko and I were walking by the East 67th Street police station a couple of nights ago, when a patrol car pulled up, and three cops hustled a hoodlum up the stairs into the station house. Just as they got to the top of the stairs, one cop pointed to the bedraggled and forlorn-looking hood, and said to me: "The Best of Paar."

I had a very large and dirty office over the lobby at the Hudson, and I soon had it wonderfully cluttered with filing cabinets, tape recorders, record players and thousands of notes tacked all over the walls. Also pin-up pictures of purple-behinded baboons and race drivers; and a few lewd friendships cards. The whole operation was very cosy and extremely inefficient. People would send us livestock; rabbits, chickens, puppies, kittens, parakeets and, every once in a while, a boa constricter—I don't know why. I think someone in the organization had, in a moment of martini-ed enthusiasm, joined the boa-constricter-of-the-month club. Anyway, they came at regular intervals, and varied in length from eight to about twelve or thirteen feet. They were harmless, as far as biting was concerned, but sometimes they were quite difficult to unwind from your arm or your leg. They were constricters, and—by God!—they were gonna *constrict!* All the livestock, including the snakes, were given to the rich or some other worthy group, but it *did* take time and quite a few bucks for feed; and the cleaning woman, Gladys, could not be persuaded, for any kind of money, to clean any snake cages. For a while there, we considered joining the mongoose-of-the-month club to sort of even things up, but nothing ever came of this, *I* thought, very sensible plan.

Something else, which was fun at first, and later turned into a plague, was the friends-of-singers organization. It was not really an organization; it just seemed like it. At first, when someone dropped in to say hello, on behalf of some singer, it broke up the monotony of the day, and gave me an excuse to knock off work for a few moments, but later on, the more popular the show became, the more popular *I* became, as the friend of the friends of singers. They were all friends of very "great" singers, and they all had "demo" records to prove this, and would I make sure that Paar listened to their record? I promised each and every one that Paar would hear their demo records as soon as I pinned him down. Actually, I never tried to pin Paar down, which is the basis of our long friendship. And if I had gotten him to listen to one of these records, what would it prove? That somebody had a good voice? So what? *Everybody* has a good voice, and not only that, most of the established singers, with LP albums in circulation, also wanted to get on the show, and they *all* had good voices; and, besides, it wasn't my department. I had nothing to do with hiring the talent. My job was writing. I made this quite clear to them, but these poor unfortunates figured that a word from me—and Paar would make them a star overnight. Personally, I think a word from me to Paar would have created a helluva unemployment problem.

One day Paar came into my office, and he seemed quite nervous. This was in the afternoon and too early to be jittery about the show, so I asked him what was wrong. He said, "I just called the producer a fag." When I didn't say anything, he said, "Did I do the wrong thing?" I waited for a minute, then I asked him, "Is he a card-carrying fag or just a plain fag?" He said, "I don't know. All I know is— he's through." Then he got up and walked out of the office. I never investigated the producer to find out if he was or wasn't, but he *was through*. It took a little time, but one day I noticed his gossamer wings were missing from the front hall tree.

CHAPTER 24

The Quick Or The Dead

THE VERY FIRST TIME I appeared on the Paar show, at one point something went wrong, and I said "Oh Jesus!" I quickly tried to cover it up by saying, "Well, there goes the Billy Graham account." Thus, within the space of about three seconds, I had lost two friends.

Since then I have been on the show about fifty times. During the early days I had quite some difficulty in being heard, mainly because I had to speak over a background of Dody Goodman. Dody may not be very clever, but she certainly is continuous. It was like swimming *down* the Columbia River while the salmon were coming *up*. Not that I think Dody is too anxious to spawn, but it's the only analogy I can think of at the moment. Nevertheless, I'm grateful to Dody, because she was unconsciously teaching me the law of survival—as pertaining to the Paar show, at any rate. You *have* to talk on the Paar show and *keep talking*. You have to jump into any conversation, with both feet, and keep on talking, whether you know what you are talking about or not; that seems to be the success formula with most of Paar's guests. It works pretty well, too, except with unusual cases, like Jack E. Leonard. Fat Jack's style precludes any *other* sound. He doesn't need a straight man. He needs an echo. A deaf echo. He's the man with a machine gun, and you're standing there with a fly swatter—in your underwear. Only once have I seen him soften up with an opponent, and that was recently when Reiko and I were on the show against him. Concerning his brusqueness, Reiko said, during a pause (a miracle in itself), "You just talk like that—you really have a warm heart." Tears immediately welled up in Fat Jack's eyes, because she was right; he *is* a very *kind* and *gentle* man. I've *never* seen him run over a dog or an old lady. The fact that he can't drive a car is beside the point.

The Paar show is not only a battle of wits, it's a battle for the opportunity to *be* a wit. I'm not speaking of sitting next to Jack and talking to him alone. I mean when you have Joey Bishop, Shelley Berman, Buddy Hackett, and Paar all on there at the same time, it becomes a contest. A real contest. Every time one of them says something funny, there are three other guys ready to jump in and say something funnier, and take it from there. God help you if you hesitate and let someone else jump in ahead of you—from then on it's like trying to get your ball back from the Harlem Globetrotters. I hope this doesn't give anyone the impression that the panelists on Paar's show are just plain rude. They're not. They're rude and *funny*.

146

When I first started to appear with Paar, NBC got quite a few letters reading, "Get that drunk *off* the show!" but there were an equal number of letters saying, "Keep that drunk *on* the show!" I hadn't had a drink in years, but I do talk with kind of a lazy drawl—mainly because I drawl and I'm lazy. People who call me on the phone don't get the impression that I'm drunk; they have a different version. They always say, "Gee—did I wake you?" Then of course I say, "No, I'm just drunk," and this seems to satisfy them.

Alexander King, who looks like he'd been sewn together by Betsy Ross, and who some comic described as the "Junkie Mark Twain," is probably the most frequent, and consistently entertaining of Paar's guests. King, one night while we were sitting around waiting to go on, suddenly belched and said, "I shouldn't be here tonight." When I asked why, he said, "Because I had a stroke yesterday." Then he belched again and when I said, "Are you all right?" the man who has proclaimed to the whole world he lives on crackers and milk alone, said, "I'm fine—I just had a salami on rye at the Stage delicatessen."

Charlie Weaver, the man in the Italian suit (he won it in a crap game with Henry Armetta), is another of Paar's most frequent guests. Long ago, when the show was new, Jack asked me if I thought Charlie would be any good as a panelist and I said no. At least my judgment was consistent. A few years earlier, I had told Desi and Lucille to forget it. And before that, I'd had a chance to buy Pepsi-Cola at a nickel a share, but I didn't think it would ever take the place of Moxie. And it never did—in my heart.

Genevieve, whose French is improving with each passing year, is another favorite guest, as is Zsa Zsa Gabor. Zsa Zsa sent me a copy of her book inscribed "To My Darling Jack Douglas—with Love." I also got a copy of the book from Gerold Frank, who wrote it for her, with the same inscription. People just *try* to make me nervous!

Jonathan Winters, whom Doctor Spock is covering in his next book *The Child from Eleven to Forty-Five*, is another Paar favorite, and a very clever one. His Playtex living face, and his uncannily accurate vocal sound effects and his bouncing-ball mind make for great fun.

Joey Bishop, who looks like the silent partner in a sex circus, is also a very clever man, although of a much different type. Joey waits until somebody says something, then *he* says something—funny. This is a good system—unless, of course, you're working with Calvin Coolidge.

Hermione Gingold, the former Archbishop of Canterbury, is a very funny woman. And there aren't very many *really* funny women in show business. There are only a few I can think of at the moment. Peggy Cass. Martha Raye. Carol Burnett. Selma Diamond. Brigitte Bardot.

But forgetting these dimpled darlings, let's get back to *me*. Before I appear on the Paar show, I make notes, usually about my family or Joe's Bar and Grill over on Eighth Avenue (or as it is known here in New York, The Avenue of the Winos); or sometimes I talk about the ballet at the Metropolitan Opera House, or some fabulous party I attended at Southampton or in a Park Avenue penthouse. Then again, sometimes I talk about something that actually *did* happen, like the crazy party that Mike Todd gave for twelve thousand people in Madison Square Garden, way back when he was married to Eddie Fisher's wife.

All my professional life, both in writing and performing,

lots and lots of experts have told me that I'm too wild, and that it's better to talk about things that people know about—you must have *down-to-earth* topics. Then they point out certain parts of my night club routine, such as when I talk about something that happened in everyday life (like my marriage to Queen Marie of Roumania and our experiences in the suburbs of Bucharest) *this*, these well meaning advisors have counseled me, people can *understand*; life in suburbia *anybody* can understand. Then they point out that Alan King has made a fortune out of talking about this single subject. And he has, too. The other day I saw him driving a Rolls Royce and towing a swimming pool.

But what I'm getting at is disagreement. I disagree with all these cockeyed theories of picking tried and true, down-to-earth, something-everybody-is-familiar-with subjects. They *do* get laughs, but you can get just as big, if not bigger, laughs from some so-called "far-out," wild stuff. For instance, I have a story about a girl getting raped on top of a sixty-two-foot flagpole. The way I tell the story: a certain Mr. William M. Pettit, thirty-three, a flagpole sitter, today faced charges of statutory rape of a fifteen-year old girl atop a sixty-two-foot flagpole. According to the charges, the incident took place while Pettit was spending sixty-five days on the pole, as an advertising stunt. His living quarters on the pole consisted of a four-by-five-foot platform, covered by an awning which he could let down around himself at night. There was no ladder, and apparently the girl was raised to the platform by a rope Pettit used to haul up food.

The incident came to light when a relative of the girl spotted Pettit on the street later, and beat him severely about the head. The girl signed a statement admitting she consented to relations with Pettit. However, in cases of statutory rape involving a minor, consent is not an issue. Her parents said they knew she had been seeing Pettit on the flagpole and had ordered her to stay away from him. Sounds like a pretty wild, far-out story, doesn't it? Something I made up—right? But it isn't. This story appeared on the front page of the New York *Journal-American*, datelined El Paso, Texas, October 22, 1958 (UPI). So you see, no matter what *some* people might think, I'm *not wild*. At least, not to the people in El Paso.

CHAPTER 25

A Python In The Men's Room

DURING THE FIRST YEAR on the *Tonight* show, a very nice man, Mr. Jay Sanford of MCA (which they say stands for Music Corporation of America, actually it *is* America) sold a book of mine to E. P. Dutton & Co. It was a book I had written almost ten years before, as a Christmas present for five hundred friends (what the hell ever happened to *them?*). The book, at that time, found much favor in Hollywood, and for years it was dragged out and read aloud at parties. This was a very flattering thing for me to hear, because I knew that the same thing used to happen to the stories of Saki, whom I admire very much.

This book which I called *No Navel to Guide Him*, a title which I know now has a deep Freudian meaning, was written as a gift, and also it was written between five and eight a.m. every morning for about two months. I had read where some not-so-eminent French novelist had written tons of novels by working only these three hours a day. I tried it, and it was marvelous—because there's nothing *else* to do between five and eight a.m. You can't call anybody. Not in *my* group anyway. The morning paper hasn't arrived yet. There are no television shows. Radio, of course, is full of jolly "hi-there-good-morning-let's-hop-out-of-bed-and-get-on-over-to-the-factory-with-a-smile-on-our-face-because-it's-a-good-day-to-be-alive-and-up-and-over-at-the-factory-making Jump-for-Joy-Jock-Straps" disc jockeys, but if you don't have to be at the Jump-for-Joy-Jock-Strap plant, you really don't need a smile on your face; and you don't need Elvis Presley's "I'm just a bleatin' cretin gettin' mah gun off at the meetin'" at that hour of the day, either. So—you sit down and you work, and I never believed it before, but after a good night's sleep your mind *is* clear. Funny, how the squares are always right.

After that Christmas when I had given *No Navel to Guide Him* away, from time to time someone would ask the obvious question, "Why don't you send it to a publisher? They'll buy it in a minute!" Well, I finally sent it to *all* the publishers—and all at the *same time*, which just wasn't being done, but *I* didn't know that. The result was that I've never seen such an avalanche of rejections. All personal (no printed forms). Some of them were mild, but mostly they were violent with outrage. "This book reads like it was written on a rainy Sunday afternoon in Philadelphia!" "What the hell is *this?*" "Wallpaper in a book! Are you nuts?" (*That* book *did* have a few pages of wallpaper stuck in it.) "How dare you send this book to a reputable publisher?" "Thanks, but no, thanks," was about the kindest rejection I got. Even though I had been turned down by every major publisher, my friends never gave up. Bob Hope, from time to time, sent six copies to Jack Goodman of Simon & Schuster. Mr. Goodman almost said yes, but finally changed his mind. So that was that. Nothing more happened until I started appearing on the *Tonight* show, and Mr. Sanford sold it to E. P. Dutton. Dutton "courageously," to use their phraseology, published it on April 1st, 1959, and the critics, with a few exceptions, were very enthusiastic. The book, now titled *My Brother Was An Only Child*, was on the best-seller lists for over six months.

I was going to title this chapter "The Wonderful World of Royalties," but I *didn't* get *rich*, because the book wasn't sold to a motion picture company, and for a very good reason, so *they* told me—it didn't tell a story, which sounds like a pretty weak excuse to me. Nevertheless, undaunted and unbusy that following summer, I wrote a sequel to *My Brother Was An Only Child*, called *Never Trust A Naked Bus Driver*, which also doesn't tell a story and also was not sold to a motion picture company. Now *this* book *does* tell a story. . . !

With two books not sold to Hollywood, and numerous appearances on the Paar show, I was in demand, especially by the Diner's Club, Hertz U-Drive, The Chase Manhattan Bank and various other *profit* organizations, so I decided to capitalize on my fleeting fame. With the generous helping hand of Mr. Jack Rollins, former manager of ungrateful folk singers and now my manager, I started to work in a nightclub called the Den. The Den was situated below the catacombs in the *lower* part of the Hotel Duane *basement*. Lenny Bruce, the Father Devine of the four-letter word, had preceded me at the Den, so the audience on *my* opening night braced itself as I walked on the stage. They needn't have. I didn't have any four-letter words in my act. Nor did I have an act. I had a few typewritten notes placed on a lectern at my side, and I would glance at them from time to time as I talked. I stayed at the Den for twelve weeks. The first six weeks I spent trying to discover what I was doing. The last six weeks I spent doing it (I think). The owner of the Den, Mr. Eddie Leipsig, was an extremely tolerant man. He didn't mind a bit when I told the audience that we'd just killed a python in the men's room, which wouldn't have been so bad, but the python had a midget in its mouth. Actually, we hadn't killed anything in the men's room larger than a water moccasin which had sneaked over from the ladies' room.

Every once in a while I would announce that there had been a cave-in, and we might all be trapped there for weeks, but not to worry about food, because the waiters were edible.

The Den is no longer in existence. It has been torn down to make room for an old Indian burial ground.

My next appearance was the Grand Central Hospital, where I was held over for seven weeks. My condition was diagnosed by three specialists as a heart attack. I'm inclined to agree.

CHAPTER 26

America After Dark, or *Stereo Drunks*

ONE OF THE DISADVANTAGES of playing in night clubs is *not* the fact that you may have one or two belligerent drunks in the audience, who suddenly decide that you're Elliot Ness and they're Frank Nitti—or vice-versa. Drunks, friendly or unfriendly, can always be handled with a kind word or an unkind check. The disadvantage is in having *admirers*—admirers who love you dearly and who have seen your act before and who always belt their next-table neighbor with their elbows and then pull the punch line to a joke, just *before* you do. Of course, to discourage this you can change the routining of your act around a bit, but this has no effect. They *still* pull the punch line—it's the *wrong* punch line, but this doesn't matter. To them it's *still* funny, so they laugh themselves into a coughing fit, and by the time they recover, you've forgotten where the hell you were in your routine, and everybody else in the place wonders what's so funny, and you don't know either. By now you've begun to notice the Great Stone Face—direct from Mount Rushmore—who is in *every* night club audience and *always* at a ringside table. The Great Stone Face just sits there and stares. Unblinking. His eyes have been sewn open. Just for *you*. And nothing you *do* or *say* gets any reaction from him.

It's a difficult thing to do, but you try to ignore him, putting him down as: someone who doesn't understand English; someone who has been using novocaine shaving lotion; or someone who has come to the club directly from an explosion. Whatever the cause, he remains in this catatonic state throughout your entire performance, but immediately you're finished, he sends a waiter to bring you to his table, buys you a drink and tells you how much he enjoyed your act. Weird? I think so.

Another type of night club customer, who is almost as distracting and frustrating to the performer as the Great Stone Face, is the Let's-Not-Looker. This type doesn't look at you *at all*, and is found mainly in the hinterlands. They go to a night club to *eat*. They'd *like* to eat and watch you at the same time, but they just happen to be facing in the wrong direction. And they can't turn around, because they're wearing steel neck braces under their Mackinaws. I usually carry a little blowgun I picked up in a Matto Grasso war surplus store, for this type. It makes them turn around all right, but you sometimes find yourself facing an audience full of coroners.

Nowadays, night clubs are pretty reliable financially, because of the American Guild of Variety Artists, the union which makes the night club owners put up a cash bond to insure the performers' pay, but it wasn't always like that. Once upon a time the safest thing to do when you were working in what you thought might be a shaky pay-off joint was to draw money every night against your weekly check. This wasn't the perfect system, by any means. I remember playing a rag-taggle night club in Houston. I smelled trouble the minute I called the club and asked what time the orchestra rehearsal was scheduled and the owner said *what* orchestra? We don't have no orchestra. We thought you was bringing one. I said no—all I had was an orchestra *leader*. He said that's good and I said whaddya mean that's good—what's he gonna wave his stick at? There was a long pause then he said: "Don't worry Kid, we'll getcha somethin'." Well, he did get somethin'—a piano player, a kazoo player and a bongo player. The bongo player was a wild-looking blonde, built somewhere in between Mamie Van Doren and the Chrysler building, with an evening gown slit down to her navel, which she'd had lowered by plastic surgery, and had a flashlight bulb screwed into it. I'm not too sure about this last, but *some*thing down there lit up. She and the two wetbacks who had been recruited for the occasion were to be my musical accompaniment. It wouldn't have been so bad, but we worked up on the back of the bar, and Miss Nympho of 1951 or Tessie and her Tantalizing Tassels, as she was known, worked right behind me. The next seven days was hell week. Every time I sang or danced or told witty stories, this bosomy buzz-bomb was right behind me, grinding, bumping and twitching. What she couldn't twitch, she'd twirl. And what she couldn't twirl, she'd jiggle. And what she couldn't jiggle didn't

157

exist. These myriad distractions were too much for my brand of entertainment. It was like giving the customers their choice of either watching the Chicago Fire or a guy in his backyard burning leaves.

This wasn't my only problem. I drew money each night, but on the last night I asked Fat Nat, the owner, if he was going to be able to pay me for the whole week? His direct answer slowed me down considerably. He said, "No." I said in that case I would not be able to do a show. I thought I had him over a barrel, because it was Saturday night and the joint was packed, and if there was no show he'd lose his shirt, but my threatening to walk out didn't scare him at all. In fact, he was so nonchalant about it, *I* began to get scared. I pictured myself being found some time later in several alleys, so I hurriedly put in a phone call from a backstage booth to a couple of my armed Texas pals, and asked them to escort me back to my motel. At the motel, my bodyguard loaded the getaway car, while I hid back in the bushes with a rifle—just in case. The next day, Bill Roberts, of the Houston *Post*, who now is a very good friend, wrote a scathing denunciation of me for walking out and leaving poor Fat Nat up the creek. But by the time the papers hit the stands I was in Buenos Aires.

The law of retribution finally caught up with Fat Nat— he later married Tessie and she tasselled him to death.

Another time, many years ago, I was booked to play a night club in Juarez, Mexico. Juarez may not be the hottest place in the world, but it'll do until all the reports are in. The night that I opened was typical, and the room I was supposed to work in had a wall fan that was like a propeller from the *Queen Mary*. I'd never seen a fan this size before or since. It was at least ten feet in diameter, and the blades could cut a quartette in half. Which is a step in the right direction. About eight o'clock the club owner, who I'm sure was Pancho Villa or a very close relative, said it was time for the floor show. I said, "Okay. You'd better turn off the fan." He said, "What?" I said, shouting to make myself heard above the grinding and clanking of the fan, "You'd better turn off the fan." He said, "We never turn off the fan." I said, "How the hell are the people gonna hear me?" and he said, "What?" I said, "Forget it!" and went on and did the show. Needless to say, the people *didn't* hear me, and after looking them over, I guess it wouldn't have mattered. Anyway, I was fired then and there. Pancho gave me eight pesos for my trouble, and that was that. I was stranded in Juarez, Mexico, with only eight pesos to my name. Not even enough to start a revolution. Not even enough to start a *crap game.* I hung around and watched the next show. Some Mexican M.C. took over for me. After the show, he was fired, too. I don't know whether he got eight pesos or not. A little later that night I thought I heard a volley of shots. I got the hell out of Juarez right then. I hope that the guy I stumbled over on my way to the border was just drunk. But I'm not too sure. Mexican M.C.'s don't have much of a union.

Sometimes, but not often, night club owners would surprise you. I once worked for Mr. Jules Podell who for the past twenty-one years has owned the famous Copacabana here in New York. When I worked for him it was in a much smaller place on East 50-something Street, I don't remember where, but I *do* remember going to work one night and finding the place locked up tight. The joint had folded and I hadn't had even a premonition. I thought, well, I'll never see my salary now, but Mr. Podell made sure that he found me and paid me. I was astounded, primarily because he *found* me. The hotel I was living in at the time was on an unlisted street, and instead of a switchboard Samuel Morse was tinkering in the lobby.

But things have changed. In the past year Reiko and I have played some wonderful places, including the "hungry i" in San Francisco, and the "Blue Angel" in New York, and the only risk a performer runs now is from his own security. Lately, quite a few of the big time night club entertainers have been walking off the floor in the middle of their acts, because of audience inattention or heckling or knocking over glasses or arguing with waiters or any of the other hundreds of distractions that can and do happen in a night club. I am in sympathy with the performer. Let's not forget that despite the veneer of superconfidence we see, most performers (underneath) are very unsure of themselves. They've *got* to be loved, and if they feel that they're not wanted, they go all to pieces, and their first thought is to run away and crawl into some nice, warm, safe place, like back into their mother's womb, where nothing can hurt them. Ever. So the next time you see some sensitive performer like Bobby Darin walk off the floor in a huff, you'll know where he's going.

CHAPTER 27

Ah So?

ON THE AFTERNOON of September 8, 1960, I was rehearsing
my night club act music with Gus Bivona and his boys at
the Slate Brothers, a night club in Hollywood. At the
same time, waiting to rehearse, a tiny Japanese girl, with
long black hair clear down to her tail, was strutting back
and forth, seemingly lost in thought, and trying to see how
many cigarettes she could smoke. Outside of noting that
she was wearing very tight toreador pants, I paid no attention to her, nor she to me. Six weeks and five days later
I had a Buddhist priest for a father-in-law.

It all started with one red rose. Every night I had dinner
alone in my quarters at the Beverly Hilton Hotel, and with
the dinner table they'd always send up a single red rose
in a small vase. One night, for no reason at all, I took the
rose with me when I went to work at the club, and gave it
to Reiko. The next night I did the same thing, and every
night after that for a week. The Japanese think we Amer-
icans are a pretty funny bunch anyway, so I imagine this

floral routine cinched it, as far as she was concerned. I mean, what the hell—how can a Japanese girl *arrange* one lousy rose?

The first time we went out together was to a Japanese picnic, which I asked her if I could go to with her. She was too embarrassed to say no, she told me later, so I was invited. The picnic was given by the Los Angeles Japanese Junior Chamber of Commerce in honor of about fifty Japanese from Japan (where else?). I mean they were not Nisei, consequently none of them spoke English, and my Japanese consisted of two words—"sessue" and "hayakawa" —so we didn't have any really big Open End sessions. But I was surprised at seeing these people laugh and play and enjoy themselves. I guess I had gotten the wrong impression from *Victory at Sea*.

A little later in the day, after a delicious lunch of raw egg sandwiches and octopus on bagel, we all sat in a big circle and played games. Reiko sang a couple of songs; then a man got up and demonstrated karaté, with volunteers from the audience. After we buried the volunteers, Reiko and I drove home. By this time I knew I liked her quite a bit, but it was hard to tell how *she* felt. She didn't speak much English and, besides, she slept all the way home.

From then on we started going to dinner together; then after the show at the Slate Brothers we would go to the Beverly-Wilshire drugstore and sit and talk over cups of tea until three or four or five in the morning. Gradually, I learned a few Japanese words and Reiko learned more English. Actually, right from the beginning we never had much trouble communicating, even though Reiko once said, "We cannot fight, because we no understand each other." One night I told her I wanted to buy her something, and asked what she would like? She said she had already picked out a friendship ring and had put a deposit on it. This rocked me a little, but I bought it for her.

By this time, we were getting to know each other very well, and the more I saw her, the more I liked her. She told me all about her family. Besides her mother and father, she has two sisters and four brothers, all living in Kanazawa, a city two hundred miles northwest of Tokyo and one of the few cities in Japan not bombed during the war. Reiko says she remembers the night the nearby city of Toyama was bombed, and it was "beautiful." She says Kanazawa wasn't bombed, because it's behind a mountain and the bombers couldn't see it.

Well, maybe Kanazawa wasn't bombed, but *I* was— *completely*—by this charming, gentle and loving little girl. We were married on the twenty-fourth of October at the Los Angeles City Hall, by a judge who completely skipped the part where the groom puts the ring on the bride's finger. When I reminded him, he said: "Say, that's a good idea—you put the ring on her finger, and say, 'With this ring I thee wed.' " After which he pronounced us man and wife for the second time. Either Jack Gold, my attorney, or Henry Slate (of the brothers) was best man. They were both there, but I don't remember which was which.

Reiko didn't tell her father, the important one in any Japanese family, that she had married me, because he hadn't wanted her to marry an American, so she wrote to him and mentioned me very casually. A little later on she sent him a copy of *My Brother Was An Only Child* and *Never Trust A Naked Bus Driver*, the two books that belong

163

in every Buddhist priest's library. Right, Mannie? After that she sent him a copy of a comedy LP album that I had made for Columbia Records and recorded at the Bon Soir, a very hip place in Greenwich Village—another *must* for a Buddhist priest with a hi-fi set. After we figured he had been softened up, Reiko put in a call to Kanazawa to break the news.

Maybe he was practicing being inscrutable, but he didn't turn a hair when she told him. Then I got on the phone and made a long speech, in Japanese (which I had learned phonetically), about how much I loved his daughter, and not to worry about her, etc. Then when I gave the phone back to Reiko, the first thing he said was, "Reiko—what's the idea? You know I don't understand English!"

During the past few months, from Reiko I've collected quite a few Japanese Confucianisms like: "Woman who looks sexy no good in a bed." "Men who talk too much—not so good lover." "Hot bath take it out tired." Then there are definitions, like a *wet* girl as opposed to a *dry* girl: a wet girl is one with compassion, and feeling, one who can cry; a dry girl is one with no emotions, no feelings, and who is just out for an easy buck. Sounds to me like it should be just the opposite, but. . . .

Our apartment in New York is furnished half Grand Rapids and half Tea House. The floor of the bedroom is covered with tatami mats which are two inches thick and are woven from rice fibers. We don't sleep on the floor (as yet), and Reiko's dressing table is covered with hundreds of kokeshi dolls. There are dolls carved from wood, and they are all sizes and shapes, and every time you open a window, the breeze scatters them all over the floor. We also have two Japanese lamps which also fall on the floor at the slightest breeze. Sometimes *I* fall on the floor at the slightest breeze. I think it's that heavy Japanese food I've been eating; every third rice kernel is made from the Third Avenue El. But being married to a Japanese girl has its advantages. What American husband has ever been interrupted in the middle of a tall tale, at a cocktail party, with, "Jack-san, don't be really-diculous!"? Who could get mad?

CHAPTER 28

The Next To The Last Chapter

LAST SUMMER IN NEW YORK was a "Summer Festival" as was *every* summer for the past five years I've lived here. "New York Is a Summer Festival" is the slogan some pixie public relations expert thought up, and I've never been able to find out what it means. It *could* mean that New York doesn't have as much cholera as Bombay during the months of July and August. Or it could mean that New York is a Summer Festival because the muggers wear sport clothes. Or then again, and this sounds more logical: New York is a Summer Festival because the guy who wrote the slogan lives in Honolulu. Anyway, New York is a Summer Festival like a Siberian salt mine is a Winter Carnival.

I don't mean there's nothing to *do* during the summer. There's plenty to do, even without going to night clubs or restaurants (they're not open in the summer anyway).

For one thing, almost every street corner in New York has free entertainment—large groups of men having air hammer contests (the one who digs up the most old pavement gets the first crack at digging up some new pavement—a worthwhile prize). Then there's old Chinatown; you can take a bus right down there and spend endless hours looking at opium dens, disguised as laundries, for the tourists. Or you can take a bus uptown and visit Grant's Tomb, a real Summer Festival item. Then you can bus back to the Seagram building, which *could* be a Summer Festival (and how!) if the Seagram people would only co-operate.

There are *endless* things (so they seem) to do in New York in the summer. If you wish, you can take a boat clear around Manhattan Island, and so what if a few drawbridges don't open in time? *Crouch* a little!

The people who *live* here in New York don't do these *fun things*, mainly because they don't seem to care. For instance, who would ever think of taking a trip to the top of the Empire State building? Nobody. Unless, of course, he wanted to drop a rock on a cop. And did any New Yorker *ever* think about taking a trip out to Bedloe's Island to see the Statue of Liberty? Or to the Museum of Natural History to see the dinosaurs? Or to Fire Island to see how the other third lives? Of course not. But people are the same everywhere. Do you think the citizens of Billings, Montana, ever drive over to take a look at the site of Custer's last stand? I don't think so, and you can't blame them because there are still a few status-seeking Indians hanging around, just in case the U.S. Cavalry *does* show up.

But getting back to the Summer Festival, Reiko and I

managed to miss most of it last summer, by going to Southampton, London and Chicago.

Southampton, a very fashionable watering place on the eastern end of Long Island, is very handy because it's only a one-hundred-mile drive from New York. Of course, it's quite a bit farther coming back, but it's a delightful, tree-shaded little village and was founded just two years after the 1620 landing at Plymouth Rock—by Pilgrims who wanted to get away weekends. At present it is populated (in the summer) by the smart New York social set, who either own their own homes there or lease them for the season. Friends are invited, or invite themselves down, as house guests for long fun-in-the-sun weekends. And they never forget to bring a six-dollar bottle of gin as a gift for their hosts. It costs the hosts only about *forty* dollars a day extra for *food, bedding, bath towels, beach towels, soap, suntan lotion, rash medicine, gas, oil, maid service,* and *more gin* for each guest, so this arrangement works out nicely—for the guests. Actually, I think it's just *thoughtlessness* on the part of the guest; I'm quite sure that if the host wound up in bankruptcy court, the guest would be the *first one* to help—with a six-dollar bottle of gin.

When *we're* in Southampton, Reiko and I usually stay with John and Camille. John and Camille own the Southampton Motel. It saves us a helluva lot of gin money.

After our Southampton vacation, we went to London to do a television show. London is quite handy to New York, too. If you clocked it, it would take less time to get to London than to Southampton, if you didn't have to drive to the airport.

In London we stayed at the Carlton Tower Hotel, which

168

is London's newest and *best* hotel, from the American point of view, because they feature fast room service. And it *is* extremely fast; you never get what you order, but—by God!—the waiter is in your room before you hang up the phone. I was quite shaken the first day in London, when Reiko came in off the balcony, shrugged her shoulders and said, "It looks just like Kansas City." She wasn't trying to be funny. To her *every* city looks like Kansas City, unless it has pagodas. Later on I took her down to show her the gay night life of Piccadilly Circus. There wasn't any—she was right. It *did* look like Kansas City. But darker.

The aim of British television seems to be unpunctuality at any price. And it succeeds admirably. Programs are timed with sundials, hourglasses and intuition. They come and go like Asiatic flu. Just when you think that's all there is— there's more. And the commercials don't interfere with the main body of the show. As a matter of fact, they don't interfere with anything. They come between shows and are just a series of pictures of different products, shown quickly, and the result is like flipping the pages of a magazine.

Sporting events hold quite an attraction for the British television viewer. On one over-abundant afternoon we watched the Women's Championship tennis matches at Wimbledon, Stirling Moss win the British Grand Prix at Silverstone, an important cricket match at Lord's and a lecture by Miss Patricia Penwick who claimed she was going to have a baby by immaculate conception. After this some British-type Mel Allen came on and said something about it didn't matter whether you won or lost, it was how you played the game. He sort of left it up in the air to which game he was referring.

The program Reiko and I were going to appear on was called "Personal Appearance." Our first meeting to discuss what we would do on the show was held at a public house named The Six Bells, on King's Road, in Chelsea. Everyone who had anything to do with the show was there: Sir Edward Pola, the producer, Sir Mark Stuart, the director, Sir Peter Knight, the orchestra leader, and Sir Bernard Carey, the set designer. With this group I felt like a serf whose crops had failed and I was there at the manor house to tell them my tithe would be a little late this year. But they were very courteous, and in no time at all I was uncomfortable.

The first meeting lasted about three hours, and not once did anyone mention the show. At the second meeting, someone mentioned the show, but it was too late. It was time for tea. At the third meeting the show was inadvertently mentioned again. It was too early for tea so we *had* to talk about it. At the fourth meeting we switched from tea to coffee. We didn't have a *fifth* meeting because we were on the air.

After London, we tried to get booked on a *Goodwill* Tour, because they paid a helluva lot more money than just a *plain* tour. But there were so *many* goodwill tours on the road that they were running out of unfriendly countries. So if we wanted to go on one, we would have to wait—at least until the State Department or whoever is in charge of this kind of thing, stirred up a little trouble in some hitherto quiet spot. We knew we wouldn't have long to wait, so we put our names on the list.

We *jetted* back from London, landing in New York without benefit of hydraulic fluid, and after a few days we *trained* to Chicago to appear in *The Teahouse of the Au-*

gust Moon at the Salt Creek Playhouse in suburban Hinsdale. Reiko played the part of the geisha girl and I played the part of the American army captain. I thought it would have been funnier the other way around, but I was alone in this.

I kept hoping, all during the opening night and the rest of the two-week run, that John Patrick, the author, wouldn't get wind of our little operation, because I changed his script around quite a bit, mostly inadvertently, when I forgot a line here and there. I don't really think I hurt it much. I merely changed the chief comedy character from Sakini, the Okinawan interpreter and general screwer-upper to me, another, but much wilder, screwer-upper. I purposely (after a while) changed the lines just to see what would come out of the other actors, and the results were hilarious most of the time, although from a writer's point of view, if someone had done this to a play of *mine*, I would have called Murder Incorporated immediately. But the play was a huge success. The reviews were glowing, and it broke all existing records, as every actor says. John Patrick got his royalties; I got my jollies; and the theatre manager was so happy about it he bought the cast a bag of hamburgers one night.

🖾 🖾 🖾 THE HAPPIEST DAY OF MY whole life took place during this last summer. That was the day Reiko announced that *she* was going to have a baby. Not that she had to *announce* it—although for a while there, before she did, I thought she was in on some scheme to smuggle Volkswagons into Japan. We didn't care whether it was a boy or a girl, before the baby was born, but Reiko insisted that it must have an *American* name. I told her it was okay with me and to go ahead and pick something she liked. In no time at all, she had come up with the two American names that she liked best—one was "Bonanza" and the other was "Palomino." I had to flip a coin.

CHAPTER 29

Old Dusty Tits
and Other Stories

As I AM WRITING this last chapter, I am also celebrating my one hundred and thirty-eighth birthday, and have just received the Tennessee Williams Award for being the world's oldest sex maniac. Like Bernard Baruch, Herbert Hoover and Shirley Temple always say, I intend to spend my birthday quietly. Later on this afternoon—if I'm still alive—my friends are giving me Julie Newmar—in a bikini—with one hundred and thirty-eight candles stuck all over her. Then I'm going to make a wish and blow out all of those hundred and thirty-eight candles—one at a time.

Julie may sue me for saying this, but I don't think so. I think she'll understand, and I hope everybody else does. I'm just stalling, because I don't want to finish this book. Not that it's been so much *fun* writing it, but it did bring back memories of a few enjoyable moments that I'd like to live over again. Of course, it brought back a few unpleasant memories, too, with moments I would *not* like to live over. Most of the problems I've had during my life have been created by *me*. Because of boredom. I think, when things are going a little too smoothly, we all have a tendency to break it up a little. I know *I* did. I also realize that sometimes I went a little overboard, too. Going way back to the time I clipped the Lynbrook High School janitor on the chin, just because he reprimanded me for some infraction. I wasn't really put out by what he said to me. I just wanted to break the monotony, and I did. Not only was I bored with tranquility but this unfortunate janitor had a real lantern jaw—it just sort of hung there. For a long time, I think—ever since I'd been going to Lynbrook High —somewhere deep inside I'd had a secret desire to belt it. I also had a secret desire to sleep with my biology teacher. I wish now that I had. Maybe I wouldn't have been expelled for belting the janitor.

Some of the other problems, interesting and otherwise, I created for myself had to do with women. The first great love of my life was Evelyn Speed (her real name), a girl from Lynbrook High School, but what made her so attractive to me was that she wasn't *local* (she came to Lynbrook from some exotic section in Brooklyn, called Brownsville) and she was *fast!* I don't know how I captured her because the sharpest guy in school, Gene Jourdan, was hot on her tail, and he had the advantage, because he was always dancing with her while I was playing drums in the band; and not only that, his family had money, and he wore golf knickers with tassels at the knees. He also had guts. But Gene didn't get her and, finally, neither did I. The last I heard, she was a schoolteacher and happily married to another schoolteacher (a male, I presume).

The second great love of my life was a dime-a-dance girl whom I met at the Star Ballroom, which used to be upstairs at the corner of Sixth Avenue and 42nd Street. Her name was Gertrude Kiley, and she was a very sexy girl and used to drive me nuts with her promises to meet me when she finished work, then not showing up. But finally she got to like me quite well and took me to meet her family, who lived in a cold-water walk-up somewhere on Tenth Avenue, which wasn't exactly next door to the Astors or the Vanderbilts, or even the Costellos, but it didn't matter to me. I was very much in love with her, principally, I suppose, because she was so unobtainable—to me, anyway. The last time I saw her was in the subway. She was with a Filipino whom she introduced as her husband. They were on their way to work—in a box factory in the Bronx.

The third, or maybe it was fourth, great love of my life (can't expect me to be chronological from here on in) was the most beautiful girl in Chicago. She was a model at the World's Fair, and her face and figure were absolutely the most exquisite I had seen, up until that time, anyway. She really was lovely, and, apparently, she thought I was the only man in the world for her. This red-hot romance lasted for about one week. That was about all I could stand. This poor beautiful creature didn't have a brain in her head. There was *nothing* we could talk about (afterwards). She was just a beautiful vegetable—so I introduced her to a band leader, and in no time at all they were married.

There was another girl that I had a mad romance with in

Chicago. I met her one night at the College Inn. She slipped me a note, and the romance was on. The only trouble with it was that in exactly one month I got a report from a private detective agency, with a complete run-down on our activities every hour of the day for the past thirty days, including, of course, her visits to my hotel room. I was nonplussed, and I asked the private eye who handed me the list, "What now?" He said, "Nothing—just stop seeing her." She wasn't married. The private investigators had been hired by her boy-friend, and all he wanted was that the affair be discontinued as of that moment. It was. I didn't know *who* her boy-friend was, but I had visions of winding up on the bottom of the Chicago River, with my slave bracelet attached to an anchor.

It was at about this time that I took an apartment with a now-famous piano player, who will have to be called "Hermie" (which wasn't his name) because of a married woman who slipped *him* a note one night. This woman fell in love with Hermie's feet. She was absolutely *stark raving mad* about his big, fat, flat feet! I used to come home *after* Hermie, and I could hear her in his bedroom, singing. Later, when I asked Hermie what was going on, he said, "She sings to my feet." It was true. Almost every night, when I came home I could hear her crooning "Brahms' Lullaby" or "Rockabye, My Baby" or even sometimes "She'll Be Comin' 'Round the Mountain." One day I asked Hermie if she had pet names for his toes. This seemed to cleave our friendship, so after a decent interval, I moved out. I never *did* find out what made him mad. Maybe *his* toes had fallen in love with *her* toes. I dunno.

I had quite an experience with another *femme fatale*,

176

while I was a dollar-a-night drummer in Oxnard. This particular "femme" was about eighty years old and had a penchant for very loose low-cut evening gowns, and at least once every half hour, while she was getting boxed out on booze at this cosy little roadside dump where I worked, she used to *fling* herself at me—while I was playing the drums. Her evening gown used to slip halfway to her waist, and her mammary glands used to fly in the breeze like two empty knockwurst casings. She was a real *Grapes of Wrath* character, and occasionally she used to sneak up behind me—put her hands over my eyes and play Guess Who?—then she'd scream with laughter when I'd say, "Old Dusty Tits?" The poor thing thought I was in love with her, and one night she asked me to marry her. When I told her I was making only a dollar a night, and tips, she said that was all right, because she practically owned the Kimberley diamond mines. I told her I'd let her know, and later that night I grabbed the last Greyhound for Los Angeles. I didn't want to get mixed up with *that* crowd. They probably would have wanted me to give up the drums.

I don't know how many of *you* have been in a house of ill repute, but *I* have. As a musician, it's part of the course. And why they call them houses of *ill* repute, I'll never know. Most of the places I knew were *famous*. But, nevertheless, this is a story about a Western band leader who was very popular for his fiddle playing, his nightly radio program called "Big Daddy Time," and for his famous Western-drawl opening line: "Howdy Folks—It's Big Daddy Time!"

One night on the road after we had finished doing a radio show in some town like Canton, Ohio, or St. Paul,

Minnesota, or wherever it was, one of the guys in the band suggested we spend a couple of hours in one of the local houses of prostitution. This was fine with most of the guys in the band, but this cornpone maestro said no, he didn't want to go, because he might be recognized, and that would be bad. After a few minutes of pointing out that there was nothing else to do in town at that hour, he said he'd go along—just for *laughs*.

When we arrived at the whore house, we were greeted warmly, because it was a lousy night for business, and twelve or fourteen musicians were an unexpected windfall. In this particular flesh parlor, all the girls sat around a large room, wearing nothing but G-strings, waiting for someone to give them the sign that they had been chosen to alleviate the loneliness that builds up in all men on the road. Or anywhere. It was pretty quiet in the room; we were all just sitting there, and none of the G-string lovelies were paying the least bit of attention to our "leader." Finally, this mass *un*-recognition was just *too* much for him, so he stood up, looked around and said, "Howdy, Folks—It's Big Daddy Time!"

Another night on the road (this time with Buddy Rogers), one of the trombone players, Jimmy Sylvan, and I were rooming together at the Deshler-Wallich Hotel in Columbus, Ohio. We were playing a week at the theatre which was right next door, so the hotel was very handy. Jimmy was a novelty in the band business—he not only smoked marijuana, but he drank gin while he was doing it. I had never seen this before or since. Jimmy was always very busy when he first checked into a hotel room, putting wet towels around all the cracks in the door and the transom, to keep the telltale smell of the weed from escaping. After this important operation was completed, he'd unwrap a bottle of gin, light up a "stick" and loll back and enjoy. This one particular night, although I never touched the Mexican Murads, I had a bottle of gin, too, so we both proceeded to fly a little. Along about four a.m. the furniture in the room began to annoy us no end. Everything was in just the *wrong* place. The beds, we decided, would look a lot better in the bathroom. This was quite a problem in logistics, but we persevered and finally got the beds into the bathroom— they were vertical, but they were in there. The desk we put where a bed had been. The telephone was now in the wrong place; it should be, we reasoned (quite logically), on the nightstand, between the beds. This took some doing, but, finally, after trying to stretch the cord so it would reach, which it wouldn't, Jimmy cut the cord with a Boy Scout axe he just happened to be carrying—and the phone wound up in its rightful place between the beds, on the nightstand, in the bathroom.

After this, we were pretty dirty, and though we felt we had not accomplished our mission, we decided we needed a shower, but we couldn't take a shower with the beds in the bathroom, so we moved the beds back out again into the bedroom, but by this time *nothing* looked right. It was just *too cluttered*. Then Jimmy made what I thought was an excellent suggestion—so we opened the window and threw out every stick of furniture in the room. It landed with a series of terrific crashes on the roof of the theatre next door. After this, we were so tired we lay down on the floor, after we found it, and went to sleep. When we woke up later that day and discovered what we had done, we were shocked silly. Walking through the lobby on the way to the theatre, we expected to be grabbed by a posse. But we weren't. And for the rest of that week in Columbus, nobody at the hotel even so much as mentioned hearing noises in the night, or anything. We started to relax a little bit, and figured either the hotel people must be real dopes or else nobody had *reported* the furniture missing from the room. It was tough sleeping on the floor every night, but it was better than being lynched. On the morning we were checking out, Jimmy and I asked the cashier for the bill. She gave us two bills—one for forty-six dollars for the room, and the other for five hundred and twenty-three dollars for miscellaneous. Just like that—no questions, no recriminations, no raised eyebrows. Just a bill for "miscellaneous." If the Deshler-Wallich Hotel in Columbus, Ohio, hasn't got anything else, it's got *class!*

In retrospect, I sometimes wish there hadn't been quite so *many* crises during my life. Maybe if there had been fewer, I'd now look less like Abe Lincoln and more like Abe Klurber (who lives next door and looks like George Washington). But I guess it's a little late to think about that. I also wish that during my life I had been nicer to some people, people like Mad Dog Coll, Ma Barker, Baby-Face Nelson and Two-Gun Crowley. Remember Two-Gun Crowley? Actually he carried *three* guns. He had the third gun strapped inside his thigh. Poor Two-Gun—you just don't *know* how many times he shot off his kneecap, just buttoning his fly.

But getting back to Lynbrook and Mrs. Finnegan and my goddam *drum*. That *drum* is what started the *whole lovely mess*. If I hadn't learned to play it, I might now look like George Washington and be the head of General Motors or Standard Oil of New Jersey, or maybe even had my very own unwanted-hair-removal salon. Who knows?

Mrs. Finnegan—about the drum. Just put it back in the attic, and while you're up there, please look around for my sister. I just remembered—the day we moved to California, she was up in the attic looking for it.